TOURISM-MARKETING PERFORMANCE METRICS AND USEFULNESS AUDITING OF DESTINATION WEBSITES

ADVANCES IN CULTURE, TOURISM AND HOSPITALITY RESEARCH

Series Editor: Arch G. Woodside

Recent Volumes:

ADVANCES IN CULTURE, TOURISM AND HOSPITALITY
RESEARCH   VOLUME 4

TOURISM-MARKETING PERFORMANCE METRICS AND USEFULNESS AUDITING OF DESTINATION WEBSITES

EDITED BY

ARCH G. WOODSIDE
Boston College, USA

Emerald

United Kingdom – North America – Japan
India – Malaysia – China

Emerald Group Publishing Limited
Howard House, Wagon Lane, Bingley BD16 1WA, UK

First edition 2010

Copyright © 2010 Emerald Group Publishing Limited

Reprints and permission service
Contact: booksandseries@emeraldinsight.com

British Library Cataloguing in Publication Data
A catalogue record for this book is available from the British Library

ISBN: 978-1-84950-900-8
ISSN: 1871-3173 (Series)

Emerald Group Publishing Limited, Howard House, Environmental Management System has been certified by ISOQAR to ISO 14001:2004 standards

Awarded in recognition of Emerald's production department's adherence to quality systems and processes when preparing scholarly journals for print

INVESTOR IN PEOPLE

CONTENTS

LIST OF CONTRIBUTORS

Patricia Canals	ESADE Business School, Barcelona, Spain
Christopher P. Dion	Boston College, Chestnut Hill, MA, USA
Kathleen J. Duggan	Vistaprint, South Boston, MA, USA
Lauren M. Fryc	Boston College, Chestnut Hill, MA, USA
Songshan (Sam) Huang	University of South Australia, Adelaide, SA, Australia
Aimée C. Kaandorp	University of Amsterdam, Amsterdam, The Netherlands
Jill Lang	Lowell High School, South Boston, MA, USA
Arch G. Woodside	Boston College, Chestnut Hill, MA, USA
Carlynn Woolsey	Boston College, Chestnut Hill, MA, USA

ix

PREFACE

Volume 4 in the series includes eight chapters. In the first chapter, Arch G. Woodside provides an extensive review of literature on measuring the influence of advertising and marketing to cause visits, expenditures by visitors, and returns on tourism advertising-marketing investments. He boldly predicts unobtrusive field experiments that measure tourism advertising-marketing influences will be adopted by destination marketing organizations before 2020.

In the second chapter, Carlynn Woolsey provides an information usefulness audit of tourism destination websites for Los Angeles, San Diego, and San Francisco. Which city's destination management organization (DMO) is doing the best job in providing information useful for potential visitors? Find out here.

In the third chapter, Kathleen Jamieson Duggan and Jill Lang examine six drivers for high-satisfaction of tourism websites and apply these drives to Maine, Massachusetts, and New York's websites. According to Duggan and Lang one these three states' DMOs is outperforming the other two in providing substantial amounts of information for visitors.

In the fourth chapter, Lauren M. Fryc examines information usefulness for three visitor websites for three European Mediterranean cities: Genoa, Marseilles, and Valencia. Find out how Valencia's DMO does so much better than Genoa and Marseilles in these comparisons by reading Fryc's contribution.

In the fifth chapter, Patricia Canals offers a performance audit of tourism websites by France, Spain, and Portugal. Which European country provides the most useful information for visitors? Canals answers this question.

In the sixth chapter, Christopher P. Dion and Arch G. Woodside ask whether or not the tourism websites of the following four countries differ in their quality and quantity of information: China, Poland, Russia, and Thailand. They compare DMO websites for the four countries as well as against the performances of the websites by the Lonely Planet.

In the seventh chapter, Aimée C. Kaandorp provides a content analysis of consumer-generated advertisements that promote visits to third places: Starbucks coffee shops and Chipotle restaurants. An intriguing study!

In the final chapter, Songshan (Sam) Huang offers a thick description of the dynamics of government's role in shaping China's domestic, inbound, and outbound tourism industry. This chapter contributes to building a behavioral theory of government–firm relationships.

Arch G. Woodside
Editor

TOURISM ADVERTISING AND MARKETING PERFORMANCE METRICS

Arch G. Woodside

ABSTRACT

Although scientific methods are available for evaluating the impact of intervention programs (e.g., plant growth of alternative seeds and soil treatments; consumer purchases of alternative prices, brands, and products; reforms such as regulations requiring wearing helmets by motorcycle riders), tourism marketing programs fail to use these methods. Traditional "conversion studies" – estimating the rate inquiries from tourism advertising convert into visitors by asking samples of inquirers if they visited – have fatal flaws in measuring whether or not the advertising caused visits to the destination that otherwise would not have occurred. The failure to stop doing traditional conversion studies to measure whether or not advertising causes visits appears to be an example of ignorance of ignorance, that is, tourism marketing executives do not have the knowledge and skills for applying effective methods to estimate the effectiveness of marketing and advertising's influence on causing visits, and they are unaware of their ignorance. What to do? New technologies in delivering advertising is decreasing the costs and efforts of using scientific methods for measuring advertising and marketing's impact

Tourism-Marketing Performance Metrics and Usefulness Auditing of Destination Websites
Advances in Culture, Tourism and Hospitality Research, Volume 4, 1–14
ISSN: 1871-3173/doi:10.1108/S1871-3173(2010)0000004005

on visits. Large, unobtrusive, scientific field experiments are appearing in the literature in the second decade of the 21st century. Good news at last?

INTRODUCTION: WHAT CEOS AND LEGISLATORS WANT TO KNOW ABOUT TOURISM MARKETING PROGRAMS

Hospitality firm chief executive officers (CEOs) (and legislators evaluating state and national destination tourism marketing programs) want to know valid answers to three questions regarding tourism marketing programs. First, is a given advertising and marketing program generating customers (visitors) who otherwise would not have come without the implementation of the program? Second, is the advertising and marketing program causing changes in visitors' behaviors during their visit to the destination (e.g., do they do more activities, stay more nights, spend more money because of their exposure/use of the destination's advertising than these visitors would have done/spent without the advertising). Third, what is the financial return of the investment in the advertising and marketing program – revenues generate minus all costs associated with implementing the advertising or the marketing program?

Sometimes scholars and residents of a destination ask a fourth question. Are tourism marketing programs more beneficial than harmful to the well-being of local residents and the destination's environment? Do we really want to attract visitors?

Achieving valid (and favorable) answers to these issues is important for securing support from CEOs and legislators of tourism marketing programs. Methods that provide unambiguous answers that achieve high validity and reliability should be helpful for securing such support – or support a decision to cancel the program or to implement different programs. Implementing such performance research methods should be helpful in designing future tourism advertising and marketing strategies that are effective in increasing visitors and generating profits (e.g., sales taxes net of advertising costs) resulting from implementing the strategies.

Following this introduction, the next section briefly reviews industry standard practices in measuring advertising effectiveness by destination management organizations (DMOs). Fatal Flaws in Conversion Studies as Indicators of Advertising Causing Visits discusses the fatal flaws of in these industry standard practices.

Additional Serious Flaws in Conversion Studies for Comparing Alternative Campaigns and Media Vehicles Performances describes serious flaws in conversion studies event though conversion studies can be useful for comparing the performances of alternative marketing campaigns, media, and media vehicles. Quasi and True Experiments Useful for Measuring the Impacts of Advertising and Marketing Programs describes quasi and true experiments that are useful for measuring the impacts of advertising and marketing programs in causing visits and revenues for a destination that would not have occurred without the advertising or marketing program.

Do Destination Marketing Websites Provide Useful Information for Their Website Visitors? shifts the discussion by asking and answering whether or not destination marketing websites provide useful information for their website visitors. Boldly Predicting the Near-Future for Designing Effective Tourism Advertising and Marketing Programs boldly predicts the near future for designing effective tourism advertising and marketing programs.

DMO Executives and Scholars Working Together concludes the discussion with an appeal to DMO executives and scholars to start working together to end the widespread condition of ignorance about how to validly measure advertising's impact on tourists' visits and revenues for destination brands – brands like France, Florida, and Florence (countries, states, and cities that instruct their DMOs to design effective strategies that attract tourists to visit).

STANDARD PRACTICES IN MEASURING TOURISM ADVERTISING AND MARKETING EFFECTIVENESS

"Conversion study" is the standard practice in measuring destination tourism advertising performance. Conversion studies usually include sending a questionnaire seven months or so after the advertising appears; the questionnaire is sent through the postal mail, by telephone, or by email to inquirers by using an address appearing in the advertising. The questionnaire or accompanying letter asks the inquirer to please respond to about 15–40 questions about their travel behavior; most conversion questionnaires focus most questions on one destination – the focal destination of the advertising. Most conversion studies identify the reason for the study in the survey or cover letter as an attempt to learn if the inquirer did or did not visit the destination since making the inquiry.

The typical conversion study reports 40–60 percent overall conversion rates of visitors from inquiries. For example, a conversion study might report that 250,000 visitors are estimated to have visited from the 500,000 inquiries received through the advertising program. The average total expenditures in the destination area for all categories asked in the survey might be $1,000 per visit. Consequently, $250 million might be reported as the total revenues generated from the advertising program ($1000 times 250,000 visiting parties). If the total advertising expenditure equals $5 million, the conversion study might include mention that the net revenue produced equals $50 for every $1 spent in the program.

Although important procedural advances improve tourism advertising conversion studies substantially (Woodside & Dubelaar, 2003), conversion studies still retain fatal flaws in reference to measuring whether or not tourism advertising causes visits and revenues that would not have otherwise been generated (Woodside, 1990). The basic research design for conversion studies remains unchanged since first appearing in the scholarly literature in articles by Woodside and Reid (1974, 1976).

FATAL FLAWS IN CONVERSION STUDIES AS INDICATORS OF ADVERTISING CAUSING VISITS

Conversion studies do not include scientifically designed equivalent comparison groups to control for sources of invalidity. Sources of invalidity include external events other than the advertising that could be the much bigger influences than exposure to the advertising on causing visits – a generally very good year for travel possible in combination with very ineffective advertising by competing destinations could be the principal causes of high conversion rates. Along with this "history" source of invalidity, Campbell and Stanley (1963) describe 17 other sources of internal and external validity that could be substantial causes for an observed outcome other than a treatment influence such as advertising's influence on visits.

Campbell and Stanley's (1963) remarkable contribution is the first to describe "quasi-experiment" in the behavioral sciences. Some quasi-experimental designs include comparison groups that are not scientifically designed to be equivalent, but the designs are still useful for ruling-out some sources of invalidity. Thus, a researcher with knowledge and skill relating to controlling for sources of invalidity describes the use of "nonequivalent control and test group designs." Campbell (1969) provides an insightful description of quasi-experiments of the impact of government programs attempting to influence citizens' behavior (e.g., government requirement for motorcyclists to wear helmets). Woodside, MacDonald, and Trappey (1997) provide details of a nonequivalent control and test group design to measure the impact of tourism literature on tourists' visits.

Scientifically designed, equivalent, comparison-groups designs include the use of control and treatment groups and random assignment of subjects to all groups. Random assignment is not the same thing as random selection. The objective of random assignment is to achieve statistical equivalence before administering the treatment to the subjects (exposing one group to advertising treatment X and a control group to placebo advertising Y).

Note that in a true experiment a proper control of subjects receives something – a placebo treatment. Having the control group receive nothing is a serious blunder because exposure alone to anything from the experimenter could be reason enough to cause the outcome under study. Thus, testing of the efficacy of Viagra's and other pills for temporarily eliminating "erectile dysfunction" and permitting sexual intercourse that includes ejaculation and orgasm among males who otherwise fail to achieve these outcomes includes a control group of men who receive a placebo (blue inert pill) and one or more treatment groups similar-looking blue pills but containing sildenafil citrate – the active ingredient that causes penis erections among certain groups of men (old guys).

The "placebo effect," also named the "Pygmalion effect" in education research and the "Hawthorne effect" in organizational studies, receives substantial in the scientific literature. The placebo effect is subjects' exposure to an inert treatment condition that results in a similar, or even better, performance than subjects exposed to the active treatment condition. Wikipedia.com includes 169 references in its discussion of placebo effects.

Wilcox and Woodside (2010) provide an example of a placebo effect in a true experiment in tourism website advertising. In the large, true, field experiment that Wilcox and Woodside report subjects exposed to the placebo advertising message opened the email message at higher rates than subjects exposed to alternative treatment advertising message. Wilcox and Woodside (2010) report that the advertising designed to cause increases in tourism-related behavior for the destination (France in the study) resulted in lower responses than the placebo advertising. Other studies report such less is more phenomena (Iyengar & Lepper, 2000).

How embarrassing is that for an advertising agency? The placebo treatment exposure outperforms the active treatment exposure! The possibility of such an outcome may be one of the reasons why advertising agency executives may be unsupportive of performing true experiments to test the efficacy of alternative advertising treatments. This possibility may be an important antecedent to the meager attention received in the advertising and marketing literature to Seymour Banks (1965) remarkably readable and yet highly technical masterpiece, *Experimentation in Marketing* – used copies of his book are on sale at Amazon.com for $200 apiece (June 2010).

ADDITIONAL SERIOUS FLAWS IN CONVERSION STUDIES FOR COMPARING ALTERNATIVE CAMPAIGNS AND MEDIA VEHICLES PERFORMANCES

Although conversion studies are invalid for learning whether or not advertising causes tourists to visit, they can be useful for comparing the performance of alternative marketing campaigns (Woodside & Motes, 1981) and media (Woodside & Ronkainen, 1982) in generating visitors and revenues and net returns. Such studies ask and answer questions concerning how many inquiries reported visits and estimated expenditures by tourists associate with the money spent on advertising campaign A versus B versus C (see Woodside & Motes, 1981, for such a study). Or, the conversion study may focus on inquiries, visits, and revenues generated through advertising in newspapers versus magazines (see Woodside & Ronkainen, 1982, for such a study). Or, the conversion study might focus on comparing visits, revenues, and net returns for magazines in specific categories (e.g., competing "shelter books") (see Woodside & Soni, 1990, for such a study).

However, in a meta-analysis, Woodside and Dubelaar (2003) provide strong evidence supporting the conclusion that most conversion studies commit two serious mistakes resulting in overestimating performances in such comparisons. First, most conversion studies identify the sponsoring brand by informing sample members that, "You wrote and asked for information about visiting [State, Province, Country X] and we want to know if did visit after receiving the literature you requested."

Making such a statement biases a conversion study in several ways. The respondents are likely to not return the survey if they did not visit following receipt of the requested information. The respondents to a request to complete a survey is likely to report more favorable responses about their visit if they do report a visit – reciprocity dictates favorable replies especially when respondents receive a package containing valuable free stuff [visitor's information guide (VIG), maps, and special offers]. Also, some respondents are more likely to report completing a trip after receiving the literature requested while they actually are responding about trips completed in years prior to asking for the literature.

Woodside and Dubelaar (2003) report the average conversion rate to be 47 percent in conversion studies that identify the destination brand sponsoring the study versus 36 percent among studies that do not identify the sponsoring destination brand. This finding supports the argument that identifying the brand sponsoring the study builds in a positive bias in responses.

Asking about consumption visits to four to seven competing destination brands reduces brand sponsor-identity bias and has the additional benefit of learning inquirers' behaviors (inquiries and visits) to competing and complementary destination brands. Woodside and Soni (1988, 1990) provide details of such a study. Also, asking about visiting several versus only one destination brand increases the likelihood that sampled inquirers visited one or more of the destination brands; thus interest in returning a completed survey increases. Woodside and Dubelaar (2003) find that response rates improve when surveys eliminate brand sponsor-identity bias; they report that the average response rates are 49 versus 59 percent with versus without sponsor-identity bias.

QUASI AND TRUE EXPERIMENTS USEFUL FOR MEASURING THE IMPACTS OF ADVERTISING AND MARKETING PROGRAMS

Campbell (1969) provides a brilliant treatise on quasi-experiments that includes several graphs representing the findings representative of different quasi-experimental designs. His discussion includes explanation of the "control series design" as a quasi-experimental design. In a control series design, measures of performance are made for several time periods before, during, and following the introduction of a new program for both the brand introducing the new program and control brands. Campbell and Ross (1968) show the impact of traffic fatalities of Connecticut's introduction of highway speeding crackdown in 1955 versus the absence of such a crackdown in four neighboring states to illustrate. Owing to history and maturation (sources of invalidity), all five states experienced decreases in traffic fatalities during 1956–1959, but the decline was much greater for Connecticut than the average of the other four states. "Impressed particularly by the 1957, 1958, and 1959 trend, we are willing to conclude that the crackdown had some effect, over and above the undeniable pseudo-effects of regression (Campbell & Ross, 1968)" (Campbell, 1969).

The Australian Tourism Commission's advertising 1984–1990 with Paul Hogan as a spokesperson inviting Americans to visit and "I'll slip an extra shrimp on the barbie for you" is viewable as a control series design – an example of a quasi-experiment design. Australia has never achieved the inquiry and visitation rates (adjusted for maturity effects) before or since the six years of advertising with Hogan as the country's spokesperson. Neighboring countries (New Zealand, Singapore, and Indonesia) did not experience similar jumps in these two impact factors.

Baker and Bendel (2005) provide supporting evidence of this campaign's positive influence, "Before the campaign, Australia was approximately number 78 on the 'most desired' vacation destination list for Americans, but became number 7 three months after the launch, and soon became number 1 or 2 on American's 'dream vacation' list, remaining in that position for most of the next two decades." Fig. 1 illustrates what the findings look like for such a control series design.

Consider a second quasi-experiment in tourism marketing evaluation. Fig. 2 shows the results of a quasi-experiment testing the efficacy of a free 130-page VIG offered each year to persons responding to Prince Edward Island's (PEI) tourism advertising. This research involved a large-scale, face-to-face, interview study with interview data collected at all PEI exit points – at the time of the study PEI had no "fixed link" (Canadian speak for bridge) and 93 percent of visitors existed by ferries and interviews were held on these ferries (see details see Woodside et al., 1997). A copy of the VIG was shown to respondents, and they were asked whether they had seen a copy before or during their visits. This design permits calculating total visit expenditures (adding up reports of accommodations, meals, activities, and travel reported expenses) for visitors with and without experiencing the VIG. The findings in Table 1 and Fig. 1 show substantially higher average total expenditures in PEI by both first-time and repeat visitors having versus not having the VIG.

Woodside et al. (1997) give estimates for the annual financial outcomes for PEI of having the VIG in PEI's tourism marketing program. The study provides evidence that responds to the continuing debate raging now in DMOs in U.S. and Canadian Provinces about whether or not paper copies of VIGs are too expensive to offer to inquirers. Should the DMO only provide an online "magazine" to inquirers? Should the DMO require a

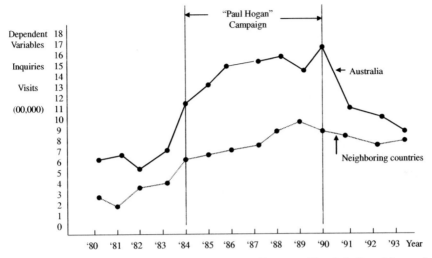

Fig. 1. Control Series Design of Advertising Effects on Tourist's Inquiries and Visits. *Note:* Fig. 1 shows a pattern of finding confirming a successful advertising strategy using a control-series quasi-experiment and not the specific findings in the Australian TV American advertising campaign for 1984–1990.

payment for a paper version of the VIG? Related questions to these VIG issues include whether or not bookings to events and for accommodations should be possible at the VIG internet site or should links only appear for such purchases.

A true-experiment design includes creating two or more groups of subjects with random assignments of subjects to groups and with one group receiving a placebo treatment and the second receiving an active-ingredient treatment (e.g., the advertising expected to cause substantial increases in inquiries, visits, and brand destination expenditures by visitors). Table 1 presents the main findings from a large-scale true experiment that included assigning 30,800 Americans randomly into one of four groups (Wilcox & Woodside, 2010). The study was designed to test the impact of offering vacation package deals to Americans to encourage visits to France. Atout France (the French government DMO responsible for promoting tourism to France) sponsored the study.

Notice in Table 1 that the presence of deals demotivates behavioral responses in comparison with the placebo treatment both in opening the email and in opening the FranceGuide.com online magazine (VIG). The net share opening both the email and the VIG marginally increases as the

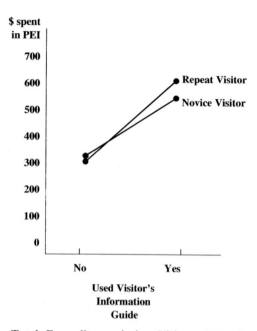

Fig. 2. Average Total Expenditures during Visit to PEI. *Source:* Data form discussion in Woodside et al. (1997).

Table 1. Findings of True Experiment for Atout France American Advertising Campaign 2010.

Advertising Treatment	% Opening (Email Opening)	% Who Opened Email (Opening FranceGuide.com)	Net %
Placebo email	19	24	4.56
2 deals email	18	7	1.26
4 deals email	17	8	1.36
15 deals email	15	12	1.80

Source: Data from discussion in Wilcox and Woodside (2010).

number of deals increases but falls well below the net share opening both in the placebo treatment group. One explanation for these findings is that the deal offers changes in the mental framing of email recipients from a friend-to-friend communication to a salesperson-to-customer communication.

Additional studies of another leisure-related industry (home gardening) indicate that focusing advertising on direct-sale offers delivers lower net returns than using a two-step approach – offering a free catalog from which customers can buy (Neubner & Woodside, 1986). The consumer research literature indicates substantial influences of mental framings on choice behavior (Woodside & Singer, 1994).

The dependent variables in the Wilcox and Woodside (2010) true experiment include behavior responses – pointing and clicking – and do not rely on self-reports by respondents. Given that most thinking occurs unconsciously (Wilson, 2002; Zaltman, 2003), self-reports often are inaccurate, and the proof is in the pudding (behavior), collecting behavioral versus verbal data alone is a substantial advance in advertising and marketing performance metrics.

Unfortunately the true experiment that Wilcox and Woodside (2010) report was not designed to test the impacts of the placebo and treatment emails on hotel and event bookings. Future research needs to include such studies.

DO DESTINATION MARKETING WEBSITES PROVIDE USEFUL INFORMATION FOR THEIR WEBSITE VISITORS?

A core issue in website advertising and marketing programs includes the three principal questions in the beginning of this chapter. The issues focus on whether or not website marketing delivers visitors and revenues net of expenses. Possibly secondary but still relevant issues are whether or not tourism websites actually contain or are perceived to contain information useful about destinations.

Woodside and Dion (2010) provide a rubric (set of rules) to measure the actual useful of tourism destination websites. Woodside and Dion use this rubric to examine the information available in the tourism marketing websites promoting visits to four countries: China, Russia, Thailand, and Poland. Their findings indicate that countries are likely to vary substantially in the usefulness of the information that they provide to travelers at websites.

A study of city tourism websites (offered by Genoa, Marseilles, and Valencia DMOs) by Fryc (2010) confirms this view for city websites as well. Valencia's tourism website outperforms the other two cities' tourism websites in providing useful information in Fryc's study.

Do tourism websites actually containing more versus less usefulness information receive more use by travelers and deliver more visits to a brand destination? This issue might be the topic of future research.

BOLDLY PREDICTING THE NEAR-FUTURE FOR DESIGNING EFFECTIVE TOURISM ADVERTISING AND MARKETING PROGRAMS

The teen years in the 21st century will bear witness to the adoption of true experiments for measuring the performance of tourism advertising and marketing programs. Advancing technologies in internet marketing will transform research relying on self-report to real-life behavior-dependent variables. Equivalent advances in tourism performance metrics are happening now that will match Gerald Eskin's (1973, 1985) accomplishments in introducing true experiments (through "single source data") of sales of frequently purchased consumer goods in supermarkets.

Coupling technological advances with theory eventually drives out ignorance of ignorance. Galileo's use of the telescope was a big boost in finally ending the widespread belief in Europe that the Sun revolves around the Earth. Internet marketing will come of age before 2020. Applications of the use of true experiments using Internet marketing platforms are doing for tourism marketing what Galileo did for astronomy.

DMO EXECUTIVES AND SCHOLARS WORKING TOGETHER

Articles appearing in the leading tourism and hospitality journals bear witness to the lack of relationships now existing between DMO executives and tourism scholars. Where are the articles having joint authors representing industry and academia?

Do not expect many joint industry-academic reports to start appearing during the 21st century teen years. However, the evidence from Galileo to Eskin indicates that a series of studies by one or small groups of individuals eventually causes big impacts on how things get measured.

What does appear likely is that hospitality CEOs and state/province legislators will continue to demand hard evidence that tourism advertising delivers visitors, expenditures by visitors, and profits for the investments made. The good news is that DMOs are finally able to deliver such evidence.

The big mistake by DMOs is still likely to be ignorance of ignorance – not knowing what you do not know about what-to-measure and how-to-measure it. The January 2009 "Management and Financial Audit of Hawaii

Tourism Authority's Major Contracts" vividly demonstrates the impact of failure of not knowing by a DMO.

> We found the HTA's [Hawaii Tourism Authority – the State of Hawaii's government office managing government tourism marketing programs] role as the lead entity and advocate of the tourism industry is significantly weakened by its inability to provide measurable results for its major marketing contractors. ... Essentially, the authority [HTA] relies on the contractors to set up their own contract terms, deliverables, and even the means by which performance will be evaluated. Lacking objective measures, benchmarks, and documentation, the authority is unable to demonstrate the effectiveness of its oversight process. In previous reports, we raised the issue of the need for HTA to develop measures that could demonstrate the effectiveness of its activities and programs. Industry experts attest to the complexity and difficulty in assessing the effectiveness of tourism development efforts such as promoting brand awareness. But absent objectively determined results, the effectiveness of taxpayer funds spent on promoting Hawaii's most important industry cannot be demonstrated. (The Auditor, 2009, pp. ii–iii)

Strong words! But similar strong words appearing in prior Hawaii tourism audit reports brought about few changes in Hawaii's measurement of its tourism advertising and marketing programs (Woodside & Sakai, 2009). Hopefully the review here will be useful for the Hawaii Tourism Authority and additional DMOs to begin to apply scientific methods now available for valid and reliable advertising and marketing performance measurement.

REFERENCES

Baker, W., & Bendel, M. (2005). Come and say g'day. *Marketing Decisions* (The Association of Travel Marketing Executives). Available at http://www.atme.org/pubs/archives/77_1898_11926.cfm

Banks, S. (1965). *Experimentation in marketing*. New York: McGraw-Hill.

Campbell, D. T. (1969). Reforms as experiments. *American Psychologist, 24*, 409–429.

Campbell, D. T., & Ross, H. L. (1968). The Connecticut crackdown on speeding: Time series data in quasi-experimental analysis. *Law and Society Review, 3*(1), 33–53.

Campbell, D. T., & Stanley, J. C. (1963). Experimental and quasi-experimental designs for research on teaching. In: N. L. Gage (Ed.), *Handbook of research on teaching* (pp. 171–246). Chicago: Rand McNally.

Eskin, G. J. (1973). Dynamic forecasts of new product demand using a depth of repeat model. *Journal of Marketing Research, 10*, 115–129.

Eskin, G. J. (1985). Tracking advertising and promotion performance with single-source data. *Journal of Advertising Research, 25*(1), 31–39.

Fryc, L. (2010). *Are tourism websites useful for travelers? Applying an information audit rubric for Mediterranean tourism destination websites*. Working Paper. Boston College, Department of Marketing, Chestnut Hill, MA.

14   ARCH G. WOODSIDE

Iyengar, S. A., & Lepper, M. R. (2000). When choice is demotivating: Can one desire too much of a good thing? *Journal of Personality and Social Psychology, 79*, 996–1006.

Neubner, K., & Woodside, A. G. (1986). *Meta-analysis of sales and profitability of direct sales versus big-book-alone advertising*. Working Paper. Park Seed Company, Greenwood, SC.

The Auditor. (2009). Management and financial audit of Hawai'i tourism authority's major contracts, report number 09-02. Honolulu, State of Hawaii. Available at http://www.state.hi.us/auditor/Reports/2009/09-02.pdf

Wilcox, C., & Woodside, A. G. (2010). *Choice conditions that motivate and demotivate response: Message relevancy, simplicity, and engagement effects on behavior*. Working Paper. Boston College, Department of Marketing, Chestnut Hill, MA.

Wilson, T. D. (2002). *Strangers to ourselves: Discovering the adaptive unconscious*. Cambridge, MA: Belknap Press of Harvard University Press.

Woodside, A. G. (1990). Measuring advertising effectiveness in destination marketing strategies. *Journal of Travel Research, 29*(Fall), 3–8.

Woodside, A. G., & Dion, C. P. (2010). *Website customer usefulness rubric*. Working Paper. Boston College, Chestnut Hill, MA.

Woodside, A. G., & Dubelaar, C. (2003). Increasing quality in measuring advertising effectiveness: A meta-analysis of question framing in conversion studies. *Journal of Advertising Research, 43*(1), 78–85.

Woodside, A. G., MacDonald, R., & Trappey, R. J., III. (1997). Measuring linkage-advertising effects on customer behavior and net revenue. *Canadian Journal of Administrative Sciences, 14*(2), 214–228.

Woodside, A. G., & Motes, W. H. (1981). Sensitivities of market segments to separate marketing strategies. *Journal of Marketing, 45*, 63–73.

Woodside, A. G., & Reid, D. M. (1974). Tourism profiles versus audience profiles: Are upscale magazines really upscale. *Journal of Travel Research, 12*(Spring), 17–23.

Woodside, A. G., & Reid, D. M. (1976). Choosing competing magazines for tourism advertising programs using a net revenue approach. *Journal of Advertising, 5*(Summer), 25–28.

Woodside, A. G., & Ronkainen, I. (1982). Inter-media comparisons of advertising effectiveness. *Journal of Advertising Research, 22*(Summer), 39–44.

Woodside, A. G., & Sakai, M. (2009). Analyzing performance audit reports of destination management organizations' actions and outcomes. *Journal of Travel & Tourism Marketing, 26*, 303–329.

Woodside, A. G., & Singer, A. E. (1994). Social interaction effects in the framing of buying decisions. *Psychology & Marketing, 11*(1), 27–34.

Woodside, A. G., & Soni, P. K. (1988). Assessing the quality of advertising inquiries by mode of response. *Journal of Advertising Research, 28*(4), 31–37.

Woodside, A. G., & Soni, P. K. (1990). Performance analysis of advertising in competing media vehicles. *Journal of Advertising Research, 30*(1), 53–66.

Zaltman, G. (2003). *How customers think*. Boston: Harvard Business School Press.

INFORMATION USEFULNESS AUDITING OF TOURISM DESTINATION WEBSITES: ASSESSING LOS ANGELES, SAN DIEGO, AND SAN FRANCISCO'S PERFORMANCE

Carlynn Woolsey

ABSTRACT

This chapter reports on how to assess the usefulness of official tourism websites; the study applies for information audit rubrics to assess the marketing websites for three cities in the state of California. The study provides tools that may be useful for designing destination websites to include information that visitors find useful. The three focal cities include Los Angeles (discoverlosangeles.com), San Diego (sandiego.org), and San Francisco (onlyinsanfrancisco.com). One of the hypotheses that the study examines is that destination websites are assessable in order of good, better, best. Findings: San Francisco provides the most useful information and is likely to be the most successful official tourism website. The assessment of San Francisco as the best website is the outcome of applying macro and micro rubrics covering: general and practical

Tourism-Marketing Performance Metrics and Usefulness Auditing of Destination Websites
Advances in Culture, Tourism and Hospitality Research, Volume 4, 15–26
ISSN: 1871-3173/doi:10.1108/S1871-3173(2010)0000004006

information, ability to book a vacation, digital and print materials, use of media components, and partnerships.

INTRODUCTION

California currently ranks as the number 1 state travel destination in the United States. According to the California Tourism Industry, the state hosted approximately 322 million (person stays to and through) domestic visitors in 2009 and approximately 13.4 million international visitors to boot (Dean Runyan Associates, 2010). In 2009, visitors spent an estimated $87.7 billion in the state of California. Travel and tourism is one of the most important industries in California. Spending by visitors generates sales in lodging, food services, recreation, and transportation. These sales support jobs for California residents and contribute tax revenue to both local and state governments (Dean Runyan Associates, 2010).

The three most visited cities in California are Los Angeles, San Diego, and San Francisco. These cities drew 42.7 million, 29.6 million, and 15.4 million, respectively (Forbes, 2010), visitors in 2009. The study here measures visitors as hotel guests, those staying with friends and relatives, those staying in accommodations outside the city but whose primary destination is the city, and regional visitors driving in for the day.

This chapter outlines the official tourism websites of each of these cities with a subsequent outline to the usefulness and overall success of each. The study applies criteria to measure usefulness building on the studies by Kim and Fesenmaier (2010) and Woodside and Dion (2010).

GENERAL WEBSITE ASSESSMENTS

Los Angeles

The official tourism website of the city of Los Angeles is describable as busy at best. The website has a white background with colorful font to match the colorful imagery cast across the homepage. The website is full of clutter with tabs that link to various points of information. The tabs, however, are difficult to navigate, resulting in an experience for which the user has to jump from link-to-link, page-to-page to find the desired information.

From a practical standpoint, the website does provide downloadable maps to visitors, as well as provides a "Visitor Resources" page should a visitor need to access a business list in the event of an emergency. The page, again however, requires a series of jumps to navigate with over 751 contacts to scroll through in a search. The Los Angeles website is translatable into the following languages: Korean, Japanese, Chinese, Spanish, and English. The website does not offer information on the local weather, which is interesting to note, given that the city is often characterizable with the prevalence of sunshine and warm weather.

San Diego

The official tourism website of the city of San Diego is designed around a theme of "Happy Happens" to depict the city as a place where fun and pleasure prevail. The website has a bright orange background with images of the beach and sunshine and surf to complement the brightness. The website is intuitive with links that are both easy-to-find and easy-to-use. The advertising on the website is minimal but effective with the main medium being a banner ad running across the top of the homepage. The banner ads are for popular area attractions. In keeping, visitors have the option to book tickets to these attractions directly, on the San Diego website. Specific attractions such as LegoLand, [the] San Diego Zoo, and Sea World, as well as general attractions such as local beaches and whale-watching expeditions are critical drivers to the tourism industry in San Diego. However, to date, the industry is experiencing year-over-year declines on account of economic and climatic conditions. Owing to El Nino weather patterns, day visitation and attraction attendance are struggling in the first quarter 2010, with both down 6.4% (San Diego Convention and Visitors Bureau, 2010).

From a practical standpoint, the website provides "Visitor Safety Tips" with important points of information. These points include information for protecting currencies and important documents, driving and parking regulations within the city, a neighborhood breakdown complete with downloadable maps, and information on visiting nearby Mexico. Given the proximity of Mexico, out of the languages the website is translatable into Italian, German, Japanese, and English; Spanish is not included. The website offers information on the local weather, complete with an extended forecast, and a surf report.

San Francisco

The official tourism website of the city of San Francisco is describable as classic and clean with an emphasis placed on conjuring the image of the iconic Golden Gate Bridge for which the city is home. The website has a white background with font and tabs that draw upon the colors of the bridge: orange, red, and rust. The website has an organization system of blocks of information, with an additional breakdown of micro-sites that are discussed in further detail at a later point in this chapter. The website allows for the option to book tickets to attractions as well as provides discount offers for these attractions.

From a practical standpoint, the website provides an "Essential ToolKit" that allows visitors to utilize interactive maps with useful information on the transportation options within the city also provided. The website has an extensive offering of emergency information with a dedicated "Personal Services" link that offers information on childcare, disabled services, and medical center resources and locations. The San Francisco website is translatable into the following languages: English, Italian, German, Spanish, French, Portuguese, Korean, Japanese, and Chinese. The website offers information on the local weather with a prominent display on the top right-hand-corner of the homepage.

BOOKING A VACATION

The study included creating the following scenario in an effort to establish the ability as well as efficiency in booking a vacation (including hotel and flight) through the tourism website for each city. Consider the following scenario for "Linda."

Linda seeks to depart from Boston on June 18, 2010, and return on June 20, 2010. The selection of this date is based on the suggestion of the Website Customer Usefulness Rubric to book a trip in mid-June 2010. Linda would like to book a hotel in the price range of $150, or under when applicable. The $150 rate should include the following amenities: exercise room, swimming pool, free Wi-Fi. Upon finding a hotel to meet these criteria, Linda would like to book a flight for this trip through the same website. Linda seeks to establish whether or not a "full" vacation can be booked on this website; is Linda able to book a vacation package or will she have to book each aspect of my vacation separately? The final piece of criteria that Linda would like to assess is whether or not she can learn what events

Table 1. Booking a Trip.

- Mock Trip Details:
  1. Can I book a trip for: June 18-June 20?
  2. Desired Hotel Rate: $150 or under
  3. Can I book a flight too?
  4. Special Events (?)

- Los Angeles
  1. BOOK IT to LA Service powered by Travelocity
  2. 48-hour sale on The Standard; $129.49 p/night; Regularly $185; 4-Star Hotel
  3. Total Price with Hotel & Flight: $439.27
  4. Events: No General Event Calendar; Must search by desired Event category

- San Diego
  1. Service Powered by ARES Travel Network
  2. Park Manor Suites; $149.25 p/night; 4-Star Hotel
  3. Total Price with Hotel & Flight: Could not book Hotel & Flight together
  4. Events: San Diego County Fair, Shakespeare Fest, Father's Day Kayaking, Padres vs. Orioles

- San Francisco
  1. Service Powered by ARES Travel Network
  2. Omni San Francisco; $141.75 p/night with 14 day advanced booking; Regularly $189
  3. Total Price with Hotel & Flight: $784.20
  4. Events: Giants County Fair, North Beach Festival, "An Evening with David Sedaris"

(if any) are occurring during the time frame of her vacation. Linda would like to achieve the latter in exploring the presence (if any) of an event calendar on each tourism website. See Table 1 for a summary of this mock trip and some key findings relating to each city.

On the basis of the information illustrated in Table 1, the only city that will meet all the criteria that Linda has, is that of San Francisco. The official tourism website of San Francisco allows for booking of a hotel at a rate less than the allotted $150, the booking of a flight in accordance with this, and has an event calendar that outlines the happenings in the city on the dates of June 18, 2010, to June 20, 2010.

DIGITAL AND PRINT MATERIALS

When visiting a city, considering what resources will be available as learning tools, and even as tools to use upon arrival, is important. The availability of a print guide is one such resource. Each tourism website champions their capacity to provide a print guide to visitors. Yet what was accessible and/or received from each city varied greatly from the information provided, as well as among each city. See Table 2 for a bulleted overview of the digital and print options listed on each website.

The Los Angeles tourism website posts a link to "Order Your FREE Visitors Guide" on the mid-section of the homepage. Upon clicking the link, a user is directed to an online order form that also includes an opt-in to receive email updates from LA Inc. (LA Inc. is the brand name denoting the Official Guide to Los Angeles). An order was placed for the guide on February 26, 2010, with contact information added to the email update database, as part of the process. Guides were ordered from each of the other cities in this study too. As of May 10, 2010, a guide from LA Inc. has yet to arrive, nor have any email updates arrived.

The "San Diego Official Visitor Planning Guide" arrived on March 12, 2010. The guide is the only option on the website that is available for mailing. The guide is part of a larger San Diego "Vacation Planning Kit." Should a user be interested, he/she has the option to download a digital version of the guide as well as a digital "Golf Guide." The website houses several other guides that are available for online viewing including: "Beach & Sea Guide," "Gay & Lesbian Travel Guide," and "Traveling with Your Pet Guide."

The San Diego "Official Visitor Planning Guide" mimics the overall "Happy Happens" campaign including a call to the campaign and sandiego.org on the cover. The cover is of a thicker paper-stock than the rest of the guide with an image of a young woman dancing on the beach. Once again the San Diego materials abound with this kind of generic

Table 2.   Digital & Print Guides.

- Los Angeles
  - Digital Guides: E-Newsletter; Active, Budget, Cultural, Family, Fashion, Gay & Lesbian, Green, Luxury, Regions
  - Print Guides: Visitors Guide

- San Diego
  - Digital Guides: E-Newsletter; Visitor Planning Guide, Digital Golf Guide
  - Print Guides: Vacation Planning Guide

- San Francisco
  - Digital Guides: Virtual Visitors Guide Winter/Spring 2010
  - Print Guides: Basic Visitor Information Kit, Gay & Lesbian Information Kit, Access Information Kit for Visitors w/Disabilities

---

imagery. Relative to the content of the guide, it is lacking in editorial. There are several activity and neighborhood breakdowns; however, the content is more relegated to that of a resource list than it is to reading material. To note about the guide is that it is from 2009. This means that the 40 coupons offered at the back of the guide are of no use, as they all expired on February 28, 2010. Aside from the resources, the only usable aspect of the guide is a pullout map. The map itself is not very detailed. It is broken out by neighborhood with prominent locations labeled. The major highways and roads are labeled but not in enough detail that a visitor unfamiliar with San Diego would be able to drive in the city.

The "San Francisco Visitors Planning Guide" arrived on March 4, 2010. The guide came as a part of a package of 3 offered on the website. The three guides are listed as follows: "Visitor Information Kit," "Access Visitor Information Kit," "Gay & Lesbian Visitor Kit." The "Access Information Kit" is of particular interest as across the cities in this study, San Francisco was the only city to offer a specific guide to visitors with disabilities. San Francisco, however, was the only city to charge for shipping of the guides too. The three guides cost a total of $14.85 for delivery through Standard US Domestic Shipping. The Standard US Domestic Shipping option was the most affordable shipping offered with the two other alternatives being a rate of $16.45 for Priority Mail or a rate of $59.69 for FedEx Standard Overnight. On the basis of the order date listed earlier, this was the most expedient delivery system for each of the three cities, as the San Francisco package was the first to arrive.

The package from the city of San Francisco was by far the best of each of the cities relative to content. The "Visitors Planning Guide" is updated quarterly, so the current guide is the Winter/Spring 2010 edition. The guide features editorial content with titles such as "High Profile, Low Profile: Visitor Favorites Meet Local Gems," "The Food Frontier: Trend Spotting on San Francisco Menus," and "10 Things to Do for $10 or Less." The content is thus interesting and informative and appeals to a range of visitors. Respective to the article titles, these visitors could be interested in topics on discovering off-the-beaten-path local establishments, the latest trends on the San Francisco food scene, or suggestions for low-cost activities, and would find all of these topics and then some, in the guide.

The guide also features a neighborhood breakdown with a pull-out map of the city included. An additional pull-out map is included in the back of the guide in a section titled "Sonoma Valley: Where to Sip and Savor in Wine Country." The map itself has prominent locations as well as popular wineries labeled. The section as a whole is presented to visitors to San Francisco whom would like to take a day trip to the nearby wine country.

An additional feature of the guide to note is a piece that is not only beneficial to a visitor but to an advertiser as well. This piece is the Business Reply Card (BRC) located on the inside back cover. This BRC links to an advertiser index that provides a number correlating to each advertiser featured in the guide. Should a visitor be interested in learning more about a particular advertiser, all he/she has to do is circle the appropriate number correlated to the advertiser on the BRC, include a return address, and drop the card in the mail. The visitor will then be contacted by the appropriate advertiser.

The San Francisco website does an excellent job in breaking down the information provided into points of interest. Particular points of interest are further broken down into micro-sites including sites for business travelers, media contacts, and a specific site dedicated entirely to dining. Taste SF is the name of the dining site. As someone who has planned entire vacations around culinary pursuits, like cooking schools, I find this site to be of particular interest. Apparently I am not alone in this type of planning either. "According to the International Culinary Tourism Association, culinary tourism is growing exponentially every year. With the steady increase in interest of food channels, travel shows featuring local and regional cuisine, food documentaries and online culinary travel shows, more consumers are traveling to various destinations just to enjoy a new food and wine experience" (Karimi, 2010).

The highlights of the Taste SF site include profiles of popular area chefs, a "Foodie Blog," as well as a "Foodie Event Calendar." A visitor to the site is also afforded the option to peruse guides to local cooking schools and/or culinary tours. The last aspect of the site – and the one that I find to be most useful – is the Restaurant Guide complete with the ability to book a reservation at a restaurant of choice. The latter is a suggested measure from the Website Customer Usefulness Rubric (Woodside & Dion, 2010), relative to the question "Can I book a classical upscale restaurant at the official website." In the case of using Taste SF, the answer then is a resounding "Yes." The Restaurant Guide is divided by category with categories that include "Brunch," "Award Winners," "Inspiring Views," and "Taste of History." These categories are not only unique yet draw upon characteristics that visitors often want but do not have the option to search for. As a final point to note, the site also has a link to "Plan Your Next Trip [to San Francisco] Today." This link directs visitors back to the booking option on the main San Francisco tourism website, making the entire booking process – from dining to vacation – near seamless.

MEDIA COMPONENTS: SOCIAL MEDIA AND VIDEO

The use of alternate forms of media is an important component to the usefulness of an official tourism website, especially in the age of new media emerging in several forms. In this case, the use of social media outlets such as Facebook, MySpace, and Twitter, and/or the use of video to showcase the city. Although each of the cities utilizes these outlets to some capacity, some applications are more useful overall than others.

The Los Angeles website offers visitors the option to follow the city on Facebook and Twitter. The website offers video in the form of a 2:15 minute video titled "LA Overview" that is essentially a scenic tour of LA with shots clipped together and compiled into one fast-paced piece.

The San Diego website offers visitors the option to follow the city on Facebook, MySpace, and Twitter. The city of San Diego wins the subsequent award for tweeting, as having followed the city, it is apparent that they tweet at a rate of at least 2–3 times per day. These tweets are an effective mode of spreading information as they often link to contests on the San Diego website or retweet information provided by the California Tourism Industry, further driving visits to the state website, as well. The website offers video in the form of television commercials available for replay.

The homepage of the website features a "Click to View Our Happy Happens Video," at the center top of the page. This video, like the four commercials provided, is full of generic imagery. The images are of children playing on the beach, children and adults alike visiting popular attractions such as Sea World and LegoLand, and of romantic sunset dining. Although these images are pleasing, they do little to differentiate San Diego from any other warm weather city. The city of Orlando comes to mind to the latter point, as like San Diego, Orlando offers warm weather and many similar attractions.

The San Francisco website offers visitors the option to follow the city on Facebook, Twitter, and YouTube. The YouTube option is of particular interest as the San Francisco website offers the most relatable content. As a promotional tool, San Francisco launched an "Escape to the City" campaign that also involved a contest. As a part of the promotion, banners were placed all over the city with the "Escape to the City" slogan emblazoned on them. Visitors and residents both were then invited to participate in a series of video shoots, posing in front of these banners and providing insight as to why they love the city of San Francisco. The responses were filmed and then later put together as a series of vignettes used to depict the campaign. The video shoot participants were subsequently invited to submit their "Escape to the City" vignettes on onlyinsanfrancis-co.com, as a part of a larger contest. Eight contest entries were selected and posted on the website as well as on the San Francisco YouTube channel, along with the original "Escape to the City" promotional video (See http://www.youtube.com/user/onlyinsanfrancisco.com). Visitors to the website were then asked to vote for their favorite video shoot. As a final component to the contest, the winners received sponsored prize packages. The grand prize package included a two-night stay at the Hyatt Regency along the Embarcadero waterfront in addition to passes to various San Francisco attractions. The grand prize package was valued at approximately $1,000.

PARTNERSHIPS

San Francisco is the only city of the three that has an exclusive partnership with a major corporation. The corporation is American Express. San Francisco offers visitors a "Best Rate Guarantee" in conjunction for booking vacation plans through their website. The guarantee mandates that should a visitor find a better rate on a hotel or on a flight, prior to their arrival, the city of San Francisco will match that rate or reimburse previous costs to account for discrepancies. This guarantee is supported by American Express, as the corporation provides visitors with exclusive deals and offers for booking on the San Francisco website, with their American Express credit card. These deals include but are not limited to a 15% discount on attraction fees, a free dessert with dinner at a partner restaurant, a $50 gift card to the Westfield Mall when booking a stay at a partner hotel. There are approximately 14 hotels currently listed as participating in the American Express promotion.

CONCLUSION

The city of San Francisco is the best official tourism website when studied in comparison to the cities of Los Angeles and San Diego on the basis of the following points as outlined in this chapter: general and practical Information, ability to book a vacation, digital and print materials, use of media components, and partnerships. The city has received numerous awards and honors to back this hypothesis. See Table 3 for a sampling of the honors and awards San Francisco won from the months June 2009 to December 2009.

Table 3. SFCB Recent (2H2009) Awards & Honors.

- October 2009 – The readers of Condé Nast Traveler magazine voted San Francisco Best U.S. City in their annual Readers' Choice Awards; San Francisco has been ranked #1 19 out of 20 years and this is the 17th consecutive year that the city has been honored with the Best U.S. City award.
- October 2009 – Cited for its significant contribution to the local economy and the recent formation of the San Francisco Tourism Improvement District, the San Francisco Convention & Visitors Bureau received an Ebbie (Excellence in Business) Economic Development Award from the San Francisco Chamber of Commerce.
- July 2009 – Corporate & Incentive Travel honors San Francisco Convention & Visitors Bureau with magazine's 2009 Award of Excellence. Subscribers who voted for those that best served their meetings and/or incentive programs selected bureaus voted to receive this coveted honor.
- June 2009 – The SFCVB has won Meetings & Conventions magazine's "Gold Service Award" for the 22nd time.
- June 2009 – As a result of a subscriber ballot vote in Association Conventions & Facilities magazine, the San Francisco Convention & Visitors Bureau was named a winner of the 2009 Distinctive Achievement Award.

The introduction section of this chapter notes that San Francisco drew 15.4 million visitors in 2009, the smallest number of visitors of the three cities in the study. Research was sought as to whether the number of visitors to a city has a direct impact on the usefulness of the official tourism website of that city; however, data to study this relationship was unobtainable. However, regardless of the number of visitors to city, San Francisco has done an excellent job in creating a useful and successful website in onlyinsanfrancisco.com.

ACKNOWLEDGMENTS

The author acknowledges and is grateful for the cooperation of individuals in developing this study and chapter. Comments by individuals Charley Detwiler and Lizzy Feinstein, to an earlier draft, were helpful in revising this chapter. The author alone is responsible for all limitations and errors that may relate to the study and the chapter.

REFERENCES

Dean Runyan Associates. (2010). California travel impacts by county: 1992–2008. *2009 Preliminary State & Regional Estimates, 3*, 12–19.

Forbes. (2010). List: America's most visited cities. Available at http://www.forbes.com/2010/04/28/tourism-new-york-lifestyle-travel-las-vegas-cities_slide_2.html

Karimi, S. (2010). What is culinary tourism? Demand media. *USA TODAY.* Available at http://traveltips.usatoday.com/culinary-tourism-1910.html

Kim, H., & Fesenmaier, D. R. (2010). Persuasive design of destination websites: An analysis of first impression. *Journal of Travel Research, 47*(1), 3–13.

Only in San Francisco: YouTube Channel. Available at http://www.youtube.com/user/onlyinsanfrancisco

San Diego Convention and Visitors Bureau. Monthly Tourism Industry Report, March 2010. Available at http://www.sandiego.org/nav/Media/ResearchAndReports#section1

The Official Guide Los Angeles. Available at http://discoverlosangeles.com/

Woodside, A. G., & Dion, C. P. (2010). *Website customer usefulness rubric.* Working Paper. Department of Marketing, Boston College, Chestnut Hill.

SIX DRIVERS FOR HIGH-USER SATISFACTION OF TOURISM WEBSITES: PERFORMANCE AUDITING OF MAINE, MASSACHUSETTS, AND NEW YORK'S DIRECT MARKETING STRATEGIES

Kathleen J. Duggan and Jill Lang

ABSTRACT

Through the use of website usability literature and tourism website analysis and experience, this theory proposes that user satisfaction on the website relates to six key drivers. The six drivers are crucial offerings of a tourism website and without successfully applying them the website may fail to meet the requirements of the end user. The six drivers for high website usability include tourist details, site appearance/usability, deals/promotions, segment marketing, foreign focus, and use of social media. This chapter puts the theory to action during an analysis of three northeastern states' tourism websites. This study analyzes the tourism websites of New York, Massachusetts, and Maine using the six key

Tourism-Marketing Performance Metrics and Usefulness Auditing of Destination Websites
Advances in Culture, Tourism and Hospitality Research, Volume 4, 27–45
Copyright © 2010 by Emerald Group Publishing Limited
ISSN: 1871-3173/doi:10.1108/S1871-3173(2010)0000004007

drivers. The analysis demonstrates areas of strength and development for each state and directly ties back to the six drivers of user satisfaction for tourism websites.

INTRODUCTION

A successful business executive is visiting a tiny village in Maine on a vacation. He pulls his yacht alongside the boat of a local fisherman. The tourist compliments the fisherman on his catch and asks how long he was out at sea that day. The fisherman replies "Not very long, I just caught enough to meet my needs and feed my family." The tourist replies, "So what do you do with the rest of your time?" The fisherman responds, "I sleep late, fish a little, play with my children, spend time with my wife, and drink beers with my friends." The tourist says, "I have an MBA from Boston College and I can help you. You should start a fishing company and sell the extra fish you catch. With the extra revenue, you can buy another boat and then another boat until you own a fleet of fishing boats. You can then leave this little village and move to New York or Los Angeles! You can manage your growing business from the city." The fisherman asks "and then what will I do?" The tourist answers, "This might take 20 years, but at that point you can retire a wealthy man, move to a house near the coast, sleep late, play with your children, catch a few fish, spend time with your wife, and drink beers with your friends."

As this story depicts, one person's vacation is another person's livelihood. This concept is particularly true for many tourists and locals of the northeastern United States. Everyday tourists flood the northeast to visit the quaint fishing towns or bustling cities that so many Americans call home. Tourists visit for many different reasons, but they all are looking for the same outcome; tourists desire smooth travel, accommodations that meet expectations, enjoyable entertainment and great memories. The best way to achieve this outcome is through extensive research of the destination. Tourism websites provide the user information and travel details that will be essential for his or her trip. The more content and valuable information a website offers, the higher the user satisfaction.

What does a tourism website have to offer for high satisfaction? What are the key drivers that will increase customer engagement with the site? How should the site speak to the user? How should the website layout and label the tourism details? What imagery and messaging should the site use to increase satisfaction? Each of these questions must be answered for a tourism website to reach optimal efficiency.

This chapter offers a formal theory of six key drivers that promote customer satisfaction for tourism websites. The report analyzes the sites of three northeastern states and compares them using the six key drivers. Clearly demonstrating the theory and offering building blocks for further analysis across tourist sites, this analysis proves valuable to any potential site designer.

In addition, the analysis sets the stage for a deeper analysis which relates the six drivers to site metrics and tangible results.

Following this introduction, second section of this chapter describes the theory in detail and supplies relevant articles for support. The third section defines the analysis of the three tourism websites and the rating method. The fourth section presents the findings across all six key drivers. The final section is a conclusion which summarizes the findings, discusses the limitations of the report and indicates the next steps for further research.

THE SIX DRIVERS OF USER SATISFACTION

The tourism website theory proposes that user satisfaction on the website relates to six key drivers. These six drivers are the most crucial elements of a tourism site and without successfully incorporating them the site will not meet the needs of most tourists.

(D1) The first driver is the tourist details on the site. The most critical elements of tourist details are their location, including the speed and ease of finding them. The theory proposes that users' satisfaction increases when details are found with speed and ease.

(D2) The home page is a crucial aspect of the tourist site because it is the jump page between what the user first sees and the details they want to obtain. The second driver is the appearance and usability of the site with an emphasis on the home page. User satisfaction increases when the site allows tourists to move seamlessly through the website and provides the functionality to make their virtual visit to the website and their physical visit to the destination easier.

(D3) The internet is known for special deals and promotions and tourist websites should be no different. Customer satisfaction relates highly to the variety, visibility and relevancy of promotions and deals on the tourism website.

(D4) Storytelling is an important part of delivering tourism details to potential visitors and delivering the right story to the right person is crucial. Segment marketing on the site allows the destination to speak with relevancy to visitors which will increase satisfaction with the website.

(D5) The fifth driver for user satisfaction involves the four million foreign tourists who travel to the United States every year. It is vital that they receive the tourist details in their native language and in a way that is easy for them to understand.

(D6) The final driver relates to the use of social media on the tourist site. This is important because it provides the user a reference outside the traditional site to view specifics about the location. Social media is a great medium for the young adult demographic and use of this tool is increasing across all demographics.

Table 1 shows the specific elements that relate to each of the six key drivers. The first driver of the theory, which speaks specifically about locating tourist details, is supported by Miller and Remington (2004). In their study they discuss how a website's information architecture and category labels enhance performance. Their research investigates the combination of clear verses ambiguous labels and wide verses deep architecture. Their report states that user performance increases on sites with a deep, rather than wide, architecture in conjunction with comprehensible labels. This finding indicates that users do not need all details on the home page as long as the labels are clear. In addition, Resnick and Sanchez (2004) perform a similar study to analyze the effect that architectural schemes and labeling have on the user's ability to find their end objective. Their report focuses on six mock health food store websites and organizes the sites using either a product- or user-centered schema.

The product-centered sites organize items by product categories, whereas the user-centered design focuses on the user's goal. Each schema has three designs with either a high, medium, or low quality of labeling. Results from the health food study show that the label quality has significant impact on the amount of time spent finding the ultimate objective. Users who see the high-quality labels have fewer errors, and find more products than users who see medium- or low-quality labels. The reason is that the users spend less time attempting to figure out what the labels mean and avoid traveling down the wrong path.

The tourism website theory relates user satisfaction with appearance and usability and specifically focuses on the home page due to Singh and Dalaj's

Table 1. Six Drivers for High-User Satisfaction Details.

Tourism Details	Appearance and Usability	Deals and Promotions	Segment Marketing	Foreign Travelers	Social Media
Special events	Home page	Discounts: hotels	Families	Spanish	YouTube
Must do attractions	Home page: first appearance	Discounts: restaurant	Kids	French	Facebook
Maps	Home page: clean	Discounts: events	Gay/lesbian	German	Myspace
Night life activities	Home page: animation	Discounts: package deals	Young adult	Italian	Picaso
Shopping	Home page: navigation	Discounts: prominence of deals on site	Senior citizen	Dutch	Fliker
Historic	Home page: contrast colors	Discounts: value	Adventurists	Japanese	Twitter
Sightseeing	Home page: search box	Advertisements: relevance	Romantic/couples	Chinese	
Lodging	Home page: intro page	Advertisements: prominence on Site	Sports enthusiasts	Arabic	
Transportation	Home page: music	Direct marketing: email	Shoppers	Bengali	
Brochure	Home page: left navigation	Direct marketing: direct mail	Food enthusiasts	Portuguese	
	Home page: right navigation	Consumer contests	Students	Russian	
	Home page: top navigation		Budget travelers	United Kingdom	
	Home page: imagery		Brides/grooms		
	Home page: seasonal relevant		Green		
	Online transactions		Conference/businesses		
	Returning to pages		Multicultural		
	Site map				
	Quick links				
	Interactive				
	Electronical postcards				
	Games				
	Videos				
	Membership				
	Registration				

(1999) research on the topic. Their findings indicate that the home page is decisive in establishing the relationship with the user because the home page is the initial impression of the organization. Lindgaard, Fernandes, Dudek and Brown (2006) find that not only does the home page need to represent the site and organization, but they need to do it quickly. Their research states that users form their overall impression of a website in less than 50 seconds, and this impression remains consistent overtime.

Geissler, Zinkhan, and Watson (2006) concentrate their study on the quantity and quality of the data on a home page. They focus on the complexity of the home page and how it relates to user attention, attitudes, and order intent. Their research suggests designing a home page around numerous working links that guide navigation, but avoid overwhelming the home page with links or graphics that cause the page to increase in length.

Many organizations offer exclusive deals and promotions on their websites that are unique to that marketing channel. If websites do not meet this expectation, customers will be dissatisfied and will begin to use other channels as a resource. To increase satisfaction, promotional offers not only need to be available, but also need to be relevant, trustworthy, and prominent. Online deals are a crucial driver to satisfaction because deals are an expectation of users and a significant contributor to customer retention.

The theory pays particular attention to the visual appearance of the website because Chen (2009) reveals in her research that sites have a range of emotions and attitudes which impact the user's attitude toward site's content, offerings, credibility, and usability. Chen's analysis indicates a high relationship between user satisfaction of a website and likelihood to purchase the product or service. The aesthetics of the site include design, imagery, and color treatments, which will all impact the users brand image of the organization. Aesthetic judgments vary from person to person due to contrasting needs, backgrounds, intellects, emotions, and other differing variables. Chen (2009, p. 1) states, "Cognitively, it is unclear whether the concept of beauty is due to pre-attentive processing or to cognitive judgments."

Pre-attentive processing is the awareness of an item before the person thinks about or focuses any real attention on the item (i.e., awareness preceding user's focused attention). Cognitive judgments are evaluations of an item based on a person's previous experiences with other similar items. This idea of pre-attentive processing or cognitive judgments relates to the fourth driver of the theory, segment marketing. The differentiation between the messaging and content on the segment is crucial to the success of a website and the user's satisfaction.

A user's engagement increases if the site speaks directly to him or her and displays imagery which supports his or her needs. Chen's remarks focus on the necessary use of relevant imagery and messaging and indicate that this is a crucial driver for satisfaction.

Foreign travelers are a single segment of users, but this report explicitly calls them out because of their unique needs over other domestic segments. Foreign travelers require information that domestic travelers do not. This information includes language translations, currency exchanges, and cultural explanations. Foreign travelers make up a large portion of total US tourists, so it is crucial that a tourist site meets their distinct needs.

The use of social media is a key driver for satisfaction because social media allows the user to interact with the site or the organization in an online environment where they feel most comfortable. The user has the option to discuss various details with other members or fans of the organization. As social media increases across all segments and demographics, it will become an increasingly more important driver of satisfaction. Supporting the site both internally and externally, social media is a great tool to attract users to the website.

UNITED STATES NORTHEASTERN TOURISM WEBSITE ANALYSIS AND COMPARISONS

Putting the tourism website theory into action, this study analyzes tourism in three northeastern states. This study strengthens the theory by employing the six drivers as tools for analysis. The three websites are New York, Massachusetts, and Maine. These states are a part of the study because they are all in the same region of the United States, and all have similar attractions and events. This is an important factor of the analysis because different locations will have varying requirements. Thus, it is ideal to analyze similar locations.

Rating Method

Table 2 outlines the rating system for the analysis. A theory criterion can receive seven ratings. The primary numerical rating is 1–5; a score of 5 is highly satisfactory and a score of 1 highly dissatisfactory. The other two possible scores are 0 (not available) and NA (not applicable). The difference between these two ratings is that a 0 is given to the theory criterion which

Table 2.   Summary of Ranking System.

Not Applicable	Not Available	Highly Dissatisfied	Moderately Dissatisfied	Neutral	Moderately Satisfied	Highly Satisfied
NA	0	1	2	3	4	5

the site does not have, but should in order to satisfy the user. A rating of NA refers to theory criterion that is interesting, but not necessary for a satisfactory tourist site. The analysis compares each site on the six drivers and then makes an overall conclusion of the three sites using all data points.

Tourist Details Results

The tourist details analysis of the Maine and Massachusetts websites produce very similar results. The Massachusetts site scores a total of 3.9 for ease in finding the tourist details and a 3.6 for content, while the Maine site scores of 3.8 for ease and 3.8 for content. Both Massachusetts and Maine score of 4.0 for the speed.

The New York site did not perform as well as the other states, with scores of 3.0 for ease, 3.1 for speed, and 2.9 for content. One reason New York does not perform as well as the other sites is because New York's home page links have ambiguous labels. New York groups many items, activities, and events into the *What to Do* link. However, the link was not clear enough and time is wasted when searching for the end objective.

In contrast, the Massachusetts site has a section called *Plan a Getaway*, and it includes links such as *Romance, Let Loose, Explore, Play, Experience, Indulge*, and *Bond*. Maine uses a similar approach to Massachusetts and labels their primary links *Lodging, Dining, Activities, Getaways, Events, Regions, Seasons*, and *Resources*. The links on New York's site were increasingly vague when it came to the events, attractions, and things to do at the location.

The Massachusetts site promotes their *must do attractions* very clearly and prominently. The home page features a link *50 Spring Adventures for $50*. This link features 50 different attractions at several locations across the state of Massachusetts. The link offers something for everyone at a very reasonable price. The Massachusetts' home page also has a large section labeled *Feature Events* which has three events on display with pictures and then a calendar indicating that the user can search for other events by date.

The Maine and New York sites have an events section. However, the section is less prominent than the Massachusetts site and is only text, whereas the Massachusetts site uses imagery.

Another area where New York falls behind the other states for tourist details is in their print materials. Maine receives five for both ease of locating the print material and speed at receiving the material. In the mail the customers receive a catalog which includes activities and events for a trip to Maine. A road map with details of Maine is also in the package. The package is very professional and the catalog is something the user can keep all season long and bring on their vacation.

Massachusetts receives a score of 2 for ease of finding the brochure and speed of receiving it. The brochure was a smaller catalog than the Maine version did not include as many attractions or a map. The Massachusetts' catalog focuses most messaging on hiking opportunities throughout the state and less on other activities. The small catalog includes a lot of advertisements which distracts from the main message and tourist details. The New York site offers to send print material. However, the material does not arrive in a timely manner, which results in low scores. View Table 3 for an overview of all the scores pertaining to tourist details. In summary, the tourist details analysis reports that Maine has the overall highest score for tourist details with 3.9, Massachusetts is a close second with 3.8 and New York falls behind with 3.0.

Table 3. Tourist Details Scores.

Tourist Details	Ease (1–5)			Speed (1–5)			Content (1–5)		
	MA	NY	ME	MA	NY	ME	MA	NY	ME
Must do attractions	5	4	4	5	4	5	5	4	4
Maps	3	1	5	4	2	5	2	1	4
Night life activities	4	2	3	4	2	3	4	2	2
Shopping	4	3	4	4	3	4	4	3	4
Historic	4	3	4	4	3	4	4	3	4
Sightseeing	4	3	4	4	3	4	4	3	4
Lodging	4	4	4	4	4	4	3	4	5
Transportation	4	4	2	4	4	2	4	4	2
Brochure	2	1	5	2	1	5	2	1	5
Average	3.9	3.0	3.8	4.0	3.1	4.0	3.6	2.9	3.8
Total average	3.8	3.0	3.9						

Appearance and Usability Results

The appearance and usability analysis reports that Maine's home page is the highest in satisfaction with a score of 4.1. Maine's scores are highest for their use of contrasting colors and bold imagery. The Maine site uses seasonally appropriate imagery that creates a vivid picture of the adventures, activities, and sights that comprise Maine. The imagery creates demand for a Maine vacation. An example of strong imagery on the Maine site is a close up shot of a basket of eggs and the caption reads "Celebrate Maine's farm fresh goodness." Another example is a child blowing dandelion seeds and the caption reads "Wonderful springtime vacation memories." These photos create and inspire emotion with the user. The site uses animation to rotate the primary image block so that different powerful pictures are shown on the site. All scores for all three sites are shown in Table 4.

The Massachusetts site scores of 3.9 for the appearance and usability on the home page. This site excels in use of contrasting colors and strong imagery (although Maine's images are superior). An example of imagery on the Massachusetts site is a family screaming on a roller coaster ride. The Massachusetts site falls behind the Maine site due to its poor use of animation, which is viewed as more of an annoyance than a positive feature. However, the Massachusetts site has a clean and simple look which makes for easy navigation.

Table 4. Appearance and Usability Scores.

Appearance and Usability	MA	NY	ME
First appearance	4	3	4
Clean/simple	4	2	4
Animation	2	3	4
Navigation	4	3	4
Contrast colors	5	4	5
Search box	4	2	4
Intro page	NA	NA	NA
Music	NA	NA	NA
Left navigation	NA	NA	3
Right navigation	4	2	NA
Top navigation	4	3	NA
Imagery	4	3	5
Seasonal relevant	4	2	4
Average	3.9	2.7	4.1

In contrast to the other two states, New York's home page scores of 2.7 for appearance and usability. This is 34% lower than the Maine site. The primary reason for the low satisfaction score on the New York site is due to the low scores for the clean/simple search box and seasonal relevance. The New York site is very busy with an overwhelming amount of imagery, some of which is too small to see clearly. An example of this is a close-up shot of a bowling ball and a waterfall. These images are too small and do not inspire the emotion of the Maine site. The search box is confusing for users because it appears in the middle of the "I love New York" logo. New York displays imagery of skis and snowy mountains during the spring months, whereas other sites are presenting fresh spring images. In summary, the scores of the state tourism sites for appearance and usability result in Maine slightly out performing Massachusetts in user satisfaction, and significantly out performing New York.

Deals and Promotions Results

The deals and promotions driver is the area that the Massachusetts and New York state tourism websites have higher user satisfaction than Maine. The scores for all three sites are shown in Table 5. The Massachusetts site scores of 3.7 because the main image on the site is promoting a special deal,

Table 5. Deals and Promotions Scores.

Deals and Promotions		MA	NY	ME
Discounts	Hotels	4	4	2
	Restaurant	4	4	2
	Events	4	4	2
	Package deals	4	5	4
	Promience of deals on site	5	5	1
	Value	4	4	3
Advertisements	Relevance	3	4	4
	Prominence on site	3	4	3
Direct marketing	Email	3	3	3
	Direct mail	3	3	3
Contest		4	0	0
Average		3.7	3.6	2.5

the *Mass $99*. This deal is highly prominent on the site and offers multiple package deals for only $99.

One of the $99 packages that the Massachusetts site offers is a windsurfing and kayak package in Cape Cod. For the sports fan, a package is available for a hotel stay and entrance to the Basketball Hall of Fame. This site also includes special discounts for students and senior citizens, which is typically 25% off the list price. Users also have the option to download a PDF file and print out a packet of deals and promotions specific to Massachusetts travel.

The New York site scores of 3.6 due to the *Find Deals* link on the top navigation bar. After clicking on this link, users are able to search for specific deals that meet their trip requirements. There is an abundance of New York promotions and deals across accommodations, travel, restaurants, and special events. An example of a package on the New York site is an Adirondack anniversary vacation package for two. The package includes two nights in a hotel, spa treatment, wine tour, picnic for two and a trip to the Finger Lakes. For the shopping enthusiast, New York offers a two day shopping package which consists of a night stay in a hotel, breakfast, and coupons to the shopper's favorite retailers. The New York site also includes advertisements on the site which are relevant to the needs of a New York tourist.

The Maine site reports the lowest satisfaction rating for deals and promotions with a score of 2.5. The Maine site does not prominently display special deals on their home page or in other areas of the site. With some searching a user may find a couple package deals; however, the promotions are more infrequent than they are on other sites. The Maine site does a great job of showing the details of their location and invoking emotions, yet the site rarely includes price, deals, or special packages in their message.

Segment Marketing Results

The Massachusetts website excels at market segmentation and reports a total average satisfaction score of 3.5. Maine and New York fall behind with total average scores of 2.9 and 1.5. The details of the scores for all three sites are visible in Table 6. The Massachusetts site has high overall satisfaction because it specifically targets many common and unique segments of the population with messaging, imagery, and content that speaks to their individual needs from a tourist site.

Table 6. Segment Marketing Scores.

Segment Marketing	On Site			Messaging			Imagery		
	MA	NY	ME	MA	NY	ME	MA	NY	ME
Families	4	3	4	4	3	4	4	2	4
Kids	4	3	5	4	2	5	5	2	5
Gay/lesbian	5	1	1	5	1	1	5	1	1
Young adult	3	0	1	3	0	1	3	0	1
Senior citizen	1	0	2	1	0	2	1	0	2
Adventurists	3	3	4	3	3	4	3	3	4
Romantic/couples	5	3	3	4	2	3	4	2	3
Sports enthusiasts	5	3	3	4	3	3	4	3	3
Shoppers	4	3	4	4	2	4	4	2	4
Food enthusiasts	4	3	5	4	3	5	4	2	5
Students	2	0	2	2	0	2	2	0	2
Budget travelers	3	3	1	2	3	1	2	2	1
Brides/grooms	4	2	4	4	1	4	4	1	4
Green	4	0	4	3	0	4	3	0	4
Conference/businesses	4	0	2	4	0	2	4	0	2
Multicultural	4	0	1	4	0	1	4	0	1
Average	3.7	1.7	2.9	3.4	1.4	2.9	3.5	1.3	2.9
Total average	3.5	1.5	2.9						

The Massachusetts site particularly excels at Gay/Lesbian, Romance/ Couples, and Sports Enthusiasts. However, they are strong in many other segments as well. On the home page, the Massachusetts site speaks to the following segments in the following ways; MAGreen: "Massachusetts is doing our part to protect our planet," LGBT: "Massachusetts is a top travel destination for everyone," Brides: "Your day, you way," Business: "Massachusetts is the place to meet and greet," and multicultural groups: "Massachusetts is a melting pot."

The Massachusetts site changes copy and imagery depending on the person they are targeting. For example, if a user is interested in shopping in Massachusetts, they can visit the *Shopping* page which displays an image of a busy shopping day in Faneuil Hall and begins the copy with "Sorry shopaholics, you won't find any relief in Massachusetts! But you will find the latest thing at our malls, great bargains at our outlets, intriguing art in our galleries, and one-of-a-kind treasures in our unique stores." This text clearly speaks to shopping enthusiast and delivers a relatable message.

Maine reports the second highest score for market segments with a score of 2.9. The Maine site performs well in the family, food enthusiasts, and adventure segments. However, the site is less successful in the young adult, gay/lesbian and multicultural segments. The segments that Maine supports have very satisfactory content and messaging, but the low overall performance reflects the quantity of marketing segments rather than the quality.

New York reports the lowest satisfaction scores for marketing segmentation with 1.5. New York has some messaging and content which speaks to families, brides, adventurists, and shoppers. However, the content and messaging is weak and they miss many large segments of the population. The Maine and New York sites are missing an opportunity to speak to customers in a more relevant and direct manner.

Foreign Focus Results

Foreign travelers make up a large portion of tourists to the northeastern region of the United States. Therefore, one of the six key drivers of satisfaction explicitly targets foreign travelers. With a total count of eight, the Massachusetts site offers the most foreign languages. The Maine site only has two languages and New York consists of three. Although the Massachusetts site has several more language options than the other sites, the translations are only on the home page and the rest of the site is in English.

The Massachusetts site does not include any additional details for the foreign traveler, such as currency exchange or local customs. The imagery is also not as vibrant as the American English version of the site. The New York site has three language translations that go across the entire site. This site also includes important travel tips for foreign travelers.

The Maine site translates the home page into two foreign languages, but the rest of the site remains in American English. The Maine site does offer brochures in the native language, which is very helpful for a foreign traveler because they can bring the printed material with them on the trip. Although the Massachusetts site has the largest count of foreign language translations, the New York site has a higher user satisfaction because it offers the translation across all pages. The full list of common foreign languages is in Table 7 with corresponding state tourism details.

Table 7. Foreign Focus Scores.

Foreign Focus	On Site			Translate the Entire Site			More Foreign Details		
	MA	NY	ME	MA	NY	ME	MA	NY	ME
Spanish	1			0					
French	1	1	1	0	1	0		1	1
German	1	1	1	0	1	0		1	1
Italian	1			0					
Dutch	1			0					
Japanese	1			0					
Chinese	1			0					
Arabic									
Bengali									
Portuguese									
Russian									
United Kingdom	1	1		0	1			1	
Total	8	3	2	0	3	0	0	3	2
Collective score	3	4	3						

Social Media Results

The northeastern tourism sites incorporate social media marketing into their websites. Maine extends their site to the most social media outlets including Youtube, Facebook, Flicker, and Twitter. The content on the site is really informative and scores 4.3 for user satisfaction; however, the social media links are not very prominent on the site. The Maine Facebook page updates daily, but the other social media outlets are not as up-to-date. An example of a message on the Maine facebook page is "Lots to see and learn at the Maine Comics Arts Festival May 22–23 on the waterfront in Portland." This example demonstrates that Maine uses Facebook as an opportunity to promote upcoming events.

Massachusetts and New York extend their sites to Facebook and Twitter, but are not on any of the other social media outlets. The Massachusetts and New York sites feature the social media links on the home page in a more prominent spot than the Maine site. In addition, the update frequency is higher than Maine. The report indicates that even though Maine has more social media connections on their site, New York and Massachusetts offer better content, messaging and update frequency, and therefore scores an overall higher satisfaction than Maine. An example of messaging on the Massachusetts Facebook page is "The Marine's are calling Boston

Table 8. Social Media Scores.

Social Media	On Site			Content			Prominence			Update Frequency		
	MA	NY	ME	MA	NY	ME	MA	NY	ME	MA	NY	ME
YouTube			Yes			5			2			3
Facebook	Yes	Yes	Yes	4	4	4	3	3	2	5	4	5
Myspace												
Picaso												
Fliker			Yes			4			2			2
Twitter	Yes	Yes	Yes	3	4	4	3	3	2	3	4	2
Average				3.5	4.0	4.3	3.0	3.0	2.0	4.0	4.0	3.0
Total average	3.5	3.7	3.1									

Common home this week! So visit and say "hi" to our heros!" New York's latest message on their Facebook page promotes one of the state's most impressive buildings. The message is "On May 1, 1931 President Hoover pressed a button in Washington, D.C. turning on the lights of the now iconic Empire State Building and officially opening it to the world. Now, 79 years later the Empire State Building is not only a world renowned icon, but also most recently a Top 10 Green New York State Destination." A full list of social media details for each tourism site is included in Table 8.

CONCLUSIONS, LIMITATIONS, CALL FOR FUTURE RESEARCH

With a score of 3.6, the state of Massachusetts reports the highest user satisfaction in accordance with the conclusions drawn by the tourist analysis report. Maine follows with a score of 3.2 and New York with a score of 3.1. A summary of the analysis is listed in Table 9. This report walks through the performance of each state tourism website and indicates the strengths and areas for development in each section.

The analysis is useful for designers and developers of the states' websites to improve the user experience and increase satisfaction. As the report indicates, each state has areas for development and can use this tool to support those efforts.

Table 9. Summary of Six Drivers for High-User Satisfaction: Original Analysis.

Summary	MA	NY	ME
Tourist details	3.8	3.0	3.9
Appearance and usability	3.9	2.7	4.1
Deals and promotions	3.7	3.6	2.5
Segment marketing	3.5	1.5	2.9
Foreign focus	3.0	4.0	3.0
Social media	3.5	3.7	3.1
Total average	3.6	3.1	3.2

Table 10. Summary of Six Drivers for High-User Satisfaction: Second Analysis.

Summary	MA	NY	ME
Tourist details	3.8	2.9	3.8
Appearance and usability	3.9	2.8	4.2
Deals and promotions	3.7	3.6	2.5
Segment marketing	3.6	1.4	2.9
Foreign focus	3.0	4.0	3.0
Social media	3.5	3.7	3.1
Total average	3.6	3.1	3.3

Second Analysis to Check for Reliability

The second author independently judged the three websites using the same evaluation instruments used by the first author. Summary scores of a second analysis appear in Table 10. This analysis uses the same scoring method as the original analysis and measures against the same six drivers and criterion details. The second analysis was essential to support the tourism website theory because if the analysis is similar then it further supports the six drivers for high user satisfaction. As seen in Table 10, the second analysis is similar to the original in most ways. Massachusetts and Maine have the same scores for total user satisfaction as the original analysis. The Maine site scores of 3.3 in the second analysis which is slightly higher than the original score of 3.2.

One specific difference between the two analyses is that the Maine site scores lower in the tourist details area because the second analyst reports confusion when looking for lodging and transportation. However, for the appearance and usability driver Maine scores 5 for first appearance because the second analyst has a higher appreciation for the colorful images.

The New York site scores lower for contrast color in the second analyst because the green color background is too bland. The two analysts report the same scores for promotions and deals but slightly differ for segment marketing. The second analyst scores the Maine site a 4 instead of 3 for sports enthusiasts segment because the kayaking message and imagery was very strong. Although a few minor differences occur between the two analyze the overall results are very similar and support each other.

The first of the two key limitations in this report is that the study does not include an actual user test of the comparative impact of the three websites. A next step is to measure the performance of each site by analyzing user engagement, session counts, unique visitor counts, and other common website metrics. Using standard deviations, correlations, and variances, these website metrics will be used to measure state tourism statistics over time. The second limitation is the lack of analysis on the success of promotions and deals on each site.

This report indicates whether or not deals are available and assigns a score which uses relevancy as the base. However, a next step is to analyze the success of the campaigns using an A/B test. An A/B test design allows the test owner to compare metrics of two different offers, or no special deal versus a special deal.

ACKNOWLEDGMENT

The authors are grateful for the time, effort, and helpful comments by Sean Duggan and Arch Woodside.

REFERENCES

Chen, J. (2009). The Impact of Aesthetics on Attitude towards Websites. Available at www. usability.gov

Geissler, G. L., Zinkhan, G. M., & Watson, R. T. (2006). The influence of home page complexity on consumer attention, attitudes, and purchase intent. *Journal of Advertising*, 35(2), 69–80.

Lindgaard, G., Fernandes, G., Dudek, C., & Brown, J. (2006). Attention web designers: You have 50 milliseconds to make a good first impression! *Behaviour & Information Technology*, 25(2), 115–126.

Miller, C. S., & Remington, R. W. (2004). Modeling information navigation: Implications for information architecture. *Human–Computer Interaction, 13*(3), 225–271.

Resnick, M. L., & Sanchez, J. (2004). Effects of organizational scheme and labeling on task performance in product-centered and user-centered retail web sites. *Human Factors, 46*(1), 104–118.

Singh, S. N., & Dalaj, N. P. (1999). Web Home Pages as Advertisements. *Communications of the ACM, 42*(8), 91–99.

ARE TOURISM WEBSITES USEFUL FOR TRAVELERS? APPLYING AN INFORMATION AUDIT RUBRIC FOR MEDITERRANEAN TOURISM DESTINATION WEBSITES

Lauren M. Fryc

ABSTRACT

Numerous travel websites have become popular in the past decade. Some destination websites allow travelers to book flights, hotels, restaurant visits, and tours. They also provide a great way for other tourists to leave feedback on the visits they had to specific travel destinations and provide other customers with reliable accounts. In this case, the theory proposes that unique offerings on a website have a greater affect on getting website visitors who are potential tourists to actually visit the website's destination. The findings show that interactive tourism websites that keep up with current technology will translate into attracting the most visitors to that specific city location. This study is unique and valuable as the analysis of the three tourism websites indicates the uniqueness of each of the three specific cities located on the Mediterranean Sea: Valencia, Marseille, and Genoa. This study provides a detailed analysis of each of the three cities' travel websites and ranks

Tourism-Marketing Performance Metrics and Usefulness Auditing of Destination Websites
Advances in Culture, Tourism and Hospitality Research, Volume 4, 47–58
Copyright © 2010 by Emerald Group Publishing Limited
All rights of reproduction in any form reserved
ISSN: 1871-3173/doi:10.1108/S1871-3173(2010)0000004008

each of the websites to evaluate which is the most reliable and most appealing to today's busy travelers. Valencia's tourism website earns "Best" of the three tourism destination websites. Marseille and Genoa's website do not offer the same caliber of information and lack the detail of Valencia's website. Valencia's website is easy to use, has the most up-to-date technology sources, and is physically the most appealing.

INTRODUCTION

New technologies are appearing in the marketplace each month early in the 21st century. Ten years ago, most people in the world did not own a cell phone; never mind a cell phone that could search the Internet, check emails, take pictures, or conference call multiple people at once. In today's ever changing society, technology, specifically with cell phone and computer applications, is something that people basically cannot live without. Consider the direction that our society is going down, in terms of a virtual society (Mlot, 2010). Will it reach a point when a person will be able to virtually experience every travel destination, and will no longer have any desire to physically travel to these historic locations?

This chapter has the following organization. This study compares three travel websites for European destinations of the Mediterranean Sea: Valencia, Spain; Marseille, France; and Genoa, Italy. Following the initial analyses of these three websites, the study compares all three websites with each other. This study includes ranking the websites using a performance audit rubric. The results may help to draw conclusions on the usefulness of each travel website for the three cities and consider the implications and affects the website has on that specific tourism market.

LITERATURE

Articles on the topic of "e-tourism" assert that not all websites are created equal, nor are all websites judged equally. Fesenmair and Kim (2008, p. 10) suggest, "When an online travel planner first evaluates the relevance and usefulness of a Web site, he or she evaluates the web site within a short period of time." This process of viewing allows the user to form "an overall impression of [the website]" simple in a matter of seconds (Fesenmair & Kim, 2008, p. 8). Because of the determination that visitors to tourism websites make a decision about that particular website very quickly, the initial home page of an e-tourism website is crucial to the success of the website. The home page must be attractive, informative, and must appeal to the sense. The website must also be "playful and enjoyable," and the website must "invite [the] browser to visit [often and...], increase their depth of exploration" (Fesenmair & Kim, 2008, p. 4).

Another major source of information for this analysis is the study done by Chulwom Kim that analyzes the e-tourism, specifically of Korea. The ideas that Kim uses to build the foundation for her analysis are extremely relevant to this study on the e-tourism websites of these three Mediterranean cities. Kim (2004, p. 1) asserts "An increasing proportion of Internet users are buying on-line and tourism will gain a larger and larger share of the online commerce market." The expansion of the online tourist markets will allow the tourism business to continue to expand in the future, since "the Internet offers the potential to make information and booking facilities available to large numbers of tourists at relatively low costs" (Kim, 2004, p. 1). The main benefits of the e-tourism are that they provide easy access to information on tourism services, provide better information on tourism services, and provide convenience for customers (Kim, 2004).

A third piece of literature in use to analyze the theory that all e-tourism websites are not created equally is the analysis by Bojnec and Kribel (2004), which discusses information and communication technology in tourism. Bojnec and Kribel analyze the affect that Internet, mobile technology, and wireless computing have on tourists who utilize these technological devices. With these devices, tourists are able to "gain immediate access to relevant information, of greater variety and in-depth than has been available previously, about destinations throughout the world" (Bojnec & Kribel, 2004, p. 445). Bojnec and Kribel (2004, p. 449) consider the idea that "potential tourists are searching for information on destinations, [including] prices, maps, driving directions, places to stay, activities to do, airline fares and schedules, entertainment opportunities, local event calendars and similar tourist information and tourist attractions."

All the different varieties of information listed in that statement can be easily communicated to the traveler on a tourism website. The amount of use that travel websites receive will only increase in the future, as a key factor to this entire study is "that [most tourism] transactions are conducted via the Internet" (Bojnec & Kribel, 2004, p. 450).

VALENCIA, SPAIN

Valencia's tourist website, entitled "VLC Valencia," can be found at the web address www.tuisvalencia.es. The first noticeable attribute about the website is that there are many bright colors and different smaller pictures on the screen. Also quite noticeable is the slogan that is largely printed atop the page: "Incredible but true." This slogan is a theme that the Valencia tourism office has created, to entice and tempt visitors to come experience all the unique and "incredible" events that a person may not be able to believe actually do exist in Valencia.

After familiarizing oneself with the main webpage, one can begin to delve into specific aspects that a common tourist might find useful on the website. The next noticeable feature of the website is the ease of use in booking a hotel room. The process is very simple. The website groups locations to stay on one's trip into hotels, hostels, campsites, apartments, and youth hostels. This is especially helpful, since all the hotels in the city are broken down further into categories based on quality ratings of stars. The process for booking a three-star hotel is found to be quite simple, as a person is guided with step-by-step directions along the way. There are many details provided about each hotel, and the entire reservation process is done on the main website. A visitor to this website is never referred to a different webpage to make the booking and is able to complete the reservation within four minutes of starting the process. The website also provides the option to receive a discounted offer to these hotels, based on the fact that the hotel booking was being done through the Valencia tourism website.

The next intriguing area of Valencia's tourism website is their many large and brightly colored advertisements for the downloadable Valencia Tourist Pack. This is a specific phone application that can be downloaded onto a tourist's cell phone. This downloading process can be done for free on the website, and boasts maps, videos, insider tips, hot spots, and other helpful information. The website also offers downloadable widgets that can be added onto one's computer. These widgets can provide updated information about traveling to Valencia that can pop up onto one's computer desktop and will have the ability to serve as a reminder to book one's trip to Valencia. This is an example of "the substantial connection between the advanced and sophisticated ICT and its extreme usefulness in the travel and tourism economy" (Bojnec & Kribel, 2004). On top of this, the Valencia Tourism webpage also provides links to their Twitter, Facebook, and Youtube web pages. It is clear that the Valencia Tourism bureau places a major emphasis on current and up to date technology, which is becoming increasingly important in today's modern society (Tarlow, 2003). Having a mobile application on a cell phone for tourists' destination is a rising trend across the globe (Ian, 2007). These types of technologies definitely appeal to the younger generation and would make a difference in a tourist's decision to choose which city to make their next travel destination (*The Earth Times Online Newspaper*, 2010).

Another major interesting attribute on the Valencia website is the detailed information they offer for handicapped travelers. There is an entire portion of the webpage dedicated to the hotels, restaurants, museums, and other popular tourists cites that are wheelchair accessible. Detailed routes are also described for wheel chair travelers, so that these handicapped visitors have the knowledge about which streets have ramps for them to travel on. Many travelers comment on the ease of accessibility they have while traveling in their wheel chairs on their trips to Spain (DeSha, 2004). The Valencia website also provides detailed information on museums and other city hot spots that have programs for those travelers who are deaf or blind.

One of the shortcomings of the Valencia website is the lack of a specific calendar of events. The website lists some major events and festivals that occur during a few months of the year, but there is currently not any calendar showing what is going on in Valencia each weekend. There is no information on weekly sporting events, concerts, or other specific local festivities. Another weakness of the website is that it did not offer to send any literature, such as brochures or maps, about Valencia through the mail. In this case, there is a possibility that the Valencia website is relying too heavily on their web applications and virtual technology. By not having literature that can be sent by mail, Valencia's travel bureau is missing out on appealing to a generation of older travelers and those travelers who do not have access to the Internet. The last flaw with the website was the lack of information on what type of visa different visitors from different countries need to obtain to visit Spain, and Valencia, specifically.

MARSEILLE, FRANCE

The website for Marseille, France, entitled "In Marseille...," can be found at the web address http://www.marseille-tourisme.com/en/in-marseille/. At first glance of this tourist website, a tourist is able to become extremely relaxed. The opening picture of the Mediterranean Sea and nearby cliff is breath taking and makes a person feel like they are right there in the scenery. This website has much less writing on the opening page and seems easier to navigate. It is much less overwhelming to have more relaxing pictures and less busy words.

One of the strongest attributes of the Marseille website is their unique feature of "A Bird's Eye View of Marseille." This feature of the website uses advanced technology through aerial photographs that allow the viewer to fly above different main sights of Marseille, including the port and town hall. This application allows the viewer to change the altitude, viewpoint, and direction of the aerial picture (Potter, 2008). It really makes a person feel like they are being able to experience the beautiful atmosphere of Marseille without having visited yet. This feature allows the possible city visitor to gain a better understanding of how the city is mapped out on the ground. Ultimately, this tool will allow a potential visitor to make a much more informed decision about whether or not the scenery and town setting calls to their personality, and whether or not they should book their vacation at Marseille. After seeing the gorgeous views of the city on the water, how could someone resist wanting to explore Marseille?

Another strong attribute of the Marseille site is the "Professionals" area they offer. This specific area of the website offers unique information for those visitors who are members of the news press, those wishing to hold conferences in Marseille, and for people holding seminars. On top of the unique attribute, the Marseille website also offers downloadable city maps that could be printed out. The website also displays some basic practical information with important phone numbers.

Of the three tourist destination websites being analyzed in this chapter, Marseille's website is the only website that offered to send visitor brochures. These brochures arrived approximately three weeks after the date they were requested. Although the opportunity to see pictures in a pamphlet is very exciting, the information from the brochures was only in French, even though a request had been made for English packets. However, even if the potential tourist had been able to read French, the packets would have been comparably much less helpful than the travel website. According to a tourism consultant,

A simple survey of brochures provides us with an example of how much tourism is tied to a mass marketing design. A perusal of travel brochures demonstrates the uniformity of these brochures, and it is not uncommon to see the same photo adorning the brochure of two different communities! In mass produced tourism, the differentiated becomes undifferentiated, and reality merges with the imagination of the brochures' writers. Misstatements or standardized statements abound in tourism brochures, leaving the reader with the belief that no brochure should be trusted and that he is traveling through virtual unreality. They included many details of local tourist cites, tours to attend in the city, and many phone numbers for hotel booking information. (Tarlow, 2003, p. 29)

Tarlow (2003, p. 29) asserts, "Destinations must become less dependent on brochures and other mass-produced and oriented forms of marketing," and instead should focus on advanced technology.

The major problem with the Marseille site is the "current events" listing on one of the website's pages. The most up to date event took place over two months prior to the analysis for this report. A minimal number of past events are even included, and no events for the future are planned or listed at the moment. This definitely does not provide any incentive to visit Marseille for a special reason, as no local festivals or special weeks are listed on the website. The only dates listed on the entire website are those for public holidays that occur annually. One other issue found about the Marseille website is that the hotel booking process sends the potential customer to an outside website to reserve a hotel room. The booking process could not be entirely done through the Marseille tourism website, which is less appealing to a busy traveler who is looking for a quick and easy process to book their vacation.

GENOA, ITALY

"GenoaTurismo" is the title of the Italian website focusing on tourism in the city of Genoa. The website, which can be found at http://www.turismo. comune.genova.it, is themed with the colors red and gold. The opening home page has three smaller photos that offer a visitor to click and begin their virtual exploration of the city of Genoa. Overall, the home page, which makes the largest initial impression on a site visitor, is underwhelming. Minimal information appears on the main page, as a visitor really has to search to start looking for information on tours and locations to visit.

However, if a person takes a time to search, the information can be found on the webpage – just not easily. Eventually a visitor will come upon a page of the website entitled "Site Map." This "Site Map" outlines all the Genoa tourism website has to offer and really should be clearly shown on the front home page.

One unique feature that the Genoa website has is the ability to increase the font size of all writing on the entire webpage. This is an excellent "ease of use" component that would greatly appeal to those with poor eyesight. This might also appeal to an older generation, who look for websites that are appealing to their needs ("Website"). Another unique feature of the website is the use of "live webcams" in a few locations in the cities. This allows a viewer of the site to see what was currently going on in the ports of

Genoa and in the downtown area. Unfortunately, the video quality is a little shaky every once in a while, with blurry screens coming up. But when the webcam worked properly, it was a successful and useful tool.

The Genoa website also offers detailed information on those students studying abroad in Genoa colleges. They also provide places where visitors could enroll in classes to learn the Italian language, while staying in their city for a longer period of time. The tourism website for Genoa also has an entire page dedicated to touring the city with small children. It provides the potential family with detailed information on museums, parks, restaurants, and other activities that are all "family friendly." The Genoa tourist office has so much information that they were even able to make an entire website completely devoted to children's tourism for the city!

One minor issue is that the Genoa website did not offer weather information on the main tourism webpage. Instead, the website boasts a link to a local weather webpage, but unfortunately this webpage is only written in the Italian language. The Genoa tourism office should really consider posting weather information in a more easily accessible manner and also so that it can be understood in many different languages.

Another small issue is that the entire website was only offered in four languages, Italian, French, German, and English. Genoa is not working to appeal to wider groups of tourists. Some areas of the website, including the Event Agenda, were only offered in Italian. This means that any potential tourists who do not speak Italian are unable to read and access what type of events will be going on in the city in the upcoming weeks. Most Americans may find this to be very frustrating, as they would want to have the most information possible about when would be the best time to book their trip abroad, based on major festivals and events.

RANKING

Applying the "Website Customer Usefulness Rubric" created by Woodside and Dion (2010), a ranking is made to compare the three different tourism websites to one another. The ranking is based on 19 specific criteria that stem from the rubric created by Woodside and Dion. This rubric is very recent and has not been used more than 10 times in any tourism studies. Therefore, the lack of experience and use of this rubric may make it a limitation to this study.

The rankings for the three websites were determined by the total number of individual winning antecedents that they received for each of the

19 criteria. Before starting to rank the websites, one must take into consideration any differences in size and population that the three cities might have.

These factors are important to note when considering the amount of visitors that the cities could hold in terms of capacity. The websites are ranked on how they had influenced the number of tourists who had attended their cities in the past few years.

It should be noted that Valencia's population is not any larger than that of Marseilles. Yet in 2006, Valencia's number of visitors was more than triple than that of Marseilles'.

The implications of this greater amount of annual visitors to Valencia can possibly be attributed to their use of technology on their website. The widget application on Valencia's website was first created in 2005. The Valencia website is clearly up to date on the newest technology. They knew that their increased offering of technology to travelers would help to make their city more appealing in comparison to other European cities. This increase in visitors due to technology can be seen when Valencia's annual visitors increased in the year 2007.

Valencia's website is by far the most user friendly. This website is easy to read and easy to navigate. Valencia's website provides the most information for a single website of the three tourism websites in the analysis. Valencia allows all bookings to be done directly on their main webpage and does not send the visitor to use any outside sources. The vibrant colors and unique photos allow for an appealing visible sensation that entices the visitor to the website to only want to pack up their bags and fly away to Valencia immediately.

After taking these factors into consideration, Valencia's website ranks the "Best." Differently, Marseilles' website earns a "Better," and Genoa's website earns a "Good." The Valencia website has 14 top-rankings out of 19 antecedents in the rubric. Marseille only receives four top-rankings. Genoa's website only earns one top-ranking of the 19 determinant categories, as their e-tourism website is the first such website created among the three in the comparison. The 14 top-ranking for Valencia show how user friendly the website is. It also shows how user friendly the website is, along with the incredible about of information that the website offers.

The e-tourism website of Valencia focuses its attention on captivating the website visitor with vibrant photos and unique website technology. Valencia's website is the only website to allow the viewer to become fully immersed into the web page, with such features as the separate children's webpage. On top of this, the online tourism office that allow the website visitor to click on many different objects in a real looking tourism office really makes the customer feel that they are having a hands on experience. This portion of the website also provides that personal touch that makes the customer feel that much more appreciated. Valencia's website is also the only website to use a slogan to entice the visitor. Valencia's slogan of "incredible but true" really captures the essence of the entire website, as the website shows so many fantastic events and opportunities that a tourist actually will have the potential to do and see, but only if they visit Valencia!

CONCLUSION AND IMPLICATIONS IN TOURISM MARKET

In today's fast paced society "our resource of time is so limited that the pleasure traveler is now forced into a stressful 'search-for-fun' vacation" (Tarlow, 2003, p. 29). E-tourism is at the brink of opportunity, since people's desire is to make marketing for tourism to be fast and easy. Potential tourists only have the ability to take a few minutes on their lunch breaks or after the kids are already in bed to find "locations that are 'real' and touch [their] emotions" (Tarlow, 2003, p. 30). The locations that are filled with culture, emotion, and excitement are the only tourist spots that have the potential of becoming major destinations.

To grab an e-tourist's attention, a tourism website must have an eye-catching home page. This home page must have bright graphics and also have information that is creatively organized, yet easy to access. Valencia's tourism website has both bright colors and an extremely large amount of information that any type of traveler would find extremely useful and beneficial. The organization of the website makes the website easy to navigate. On top of these features, the Valencia website is thinking far ahead into the future, with the use of their cell phone applications and computer widgets. The tourism council of Valencia realizes that the e-tourism market is one that is ever-expanding, and to increase the frequency of visitors to their city, they must make the information about the city accessible. By having downloadable applications with ideas about what great sights and events Valencia has to offer to tourists, a potential tourist will be constantly reminded about the city of Valencia. This constant reminder on one's cell phone has a higher potential to turn into an actual visit to the city of Valencia the ultimate goal of the tourism website.

Today, Valencia is not only the third most popular tourist destination in Spain but also one of the most booming cities in Europe. The city has become a firm reference, not only for other tourist destinations, but also in the academic world, with a large number of universities contacting us for information to help them write papers and thesis about the developments here. Valencia should continue to focus their efforts in the tourism market on customer retention. They should also try to develop and manage their own digital brand. As Kim asserts "brand power is more important on [the internet] than off line because the main stage of e-business is the virtual world where consumers are more dependent on recognized brands" (Kim, 2004, p. 10). Valencia has a great opportunity to expand and become the most visited city in Spain. The website will be successful if the website continues to market the brand image of an "incredible, but true" city to the entire world.

ACKNOWLEDGMENTS

The author acknowledges the helpful comments by her parents, Robert and Susan Fryc, her brother, Bryan Fryc, and Arch G. Woodside to an early draft of this chapter.

REFERENCES

Bojnec, Š., & Kribel, Z. (2004). *Information and communication technology in tourism.* Slovenia: University of Primorska.

DeSha, M. E. (2004). Wheelchair accessible travel in Spain for disabled people. *Global Access News Disabled Travel Network.* Available at http://www.globalaccessnews.com/spain04.htm. Retrieved on April 26, 2010.

Fesenmair, D. R., & Kim, H. (2008). Persuasive design of destination web sites: An analysis of first impression. *Journal of Travel Research, 47*(3), 1–15.

Ian, S. (2007). Holiday bookings through 'smartphone', a new trend: Study. *India News; Indian Business, Finance News; Sports: Cricket India; Bollywood, Tamil, Telugu Movies; Astrology, Indian Recipes.* Available at http://sify.com/news/holiday-bookings-through-smartphone-a-new-trend-study-news-international-keeiOcccibf.html. Retrieved on April 26, 2010.

Kim, C. (2004). *E-touism: An innovative approach for the Small and Medium-Sized Tourism Enterprises (S.M.I.T.E.S) in Korea.* Korea: College of Hotel & Tourism Management, Kyunghee University.

Mlot, S. (2010). Welcome center's closing could hurt thurmont businesses-Wtop.com. *WTOP.com.* Available at http://www.wtop.com/?nid = 598&sid = 1924706. Retrieved on April 27, 2010.

Potter, N. (2008). Google earth dives deeper, expands ocean feature-ABC News. *ABCNews. com-Breaking News, Politics, Online News, World News, Feature Stories, Celebrity Interviews and More-ABC News.* Available at http://abcnews.go.com/Technology/ Green/google-earth-dives-deeper-expands-ocean-feature/story?id = 10319981. Retrieved on April 28, 2010.

Tarlow, P. (2003). Tourism in a postenchanted world: New ideas, new strategies. *E-Review of Tourism Research, 2,* 1–4. Available at http://ertr.tamu.edu/attachments/140_c-1-2-3. pdf. Retrieved on April 27, 2010.

The Earth Times Online Newspaper. (2010). Aristotle launches first state tourism IPhone App; Earth Times News. *The Earth Times Online Newspaper, Serving the Planet with Breaking News,* April 26. Available at http://www.earthtimes.org/articles/show/aristotle-launches-first-state-tourism-iphone-app,1246741.shtml

Woodside, A. G., & Dion, C. P. (2010). *Website customer usefulness rubric.* Chestnut Hill, MA: Boston College.

PERFORMANCE AUDITING OF TOURISM WEBSITES: FRANCE, SPAIN, AND PORTUGAL

Patricia Canals

ABSTRACT

Measuring and evaluating the effectiveness of a website can be very difficult and subjective. These sites can be evaluated in different ways, depending on which factor is considered as the most important one in promoting a website. Theory suggests some key factors when evaluating the effectiveness of a Web site, such as the quantity of information provided, the design of the Web site, or the reciprocity created with the customer. This chapter focuses on these factors to evaluate effectiveness. However, to complete this evaluation, it is highly recommended using other traditional tools like survey methodology. Both online and email surveys are necessary to get a more detailed conclusion when investigating effectiveness of a tourism promotional Web site. Evaluation of Web site effectiveness is necessary because of the significant costs for setup, advertising, and maintenance.

INTRODUCTION

This chapter has the objective of evaluating how effective are the tourism Web sites of France, Spain, and Portugal in promoting their destinations.

Tourism-Marketing Performance Metrics and Usefulness Auditing of Destination Websites
Advances in Culture, Tourism and Hospitality Research, Volume 4, 59–68
Copyright © 2010 by Emerald Group Publishing Limited
All rights of reproduction in any form reserved
ISSN: 1871-3173/doi:10.1108/S1871-3173(2010)0000004009

Although the difficulty of measuring that, some key factors are indispensable and helpful in this process.

Section Tourism through the Internet refers to e-tourism. The Internet increasingly has become an important medium for marketing because it offers enormous potential, and it is ideal for marketing tourism (Bowen, Kotler, & Makens, 2010). Furthermore, this medium has several advantages, like more addressability, interactivity, flexibility, accessibility, improved service, and cost and time savings.

Sections Method analyses the content of the official tourism Web sites of France, Spain, and Portugal, paying special attention in the applications and opportunities that these pages offer to customers and users. The Web sites are evaluated in terms of some key factors such as the quantity and quality of information, the ability of the web page for being inspirational and reciprocal as well as the correspondence between what clients want and what these Web sites offer in their homepages.

Conclusions section concludes the study by analysis which Web site is the best one in terms of promoting its destinations. However, this study has some weaknesses, because it does not study what clients think about these Web sites. This negative point will be solved by applying special surveys oriented to study consumers' behaviors about these tourism Web sites.

TOURISM THROUGH THE INTERNET

E-tourism is a form of travel technology with a particular focus on the tourism industry (Tourism Marketing on the Internet). It means fast communications, global accessibility, and minimal costs for new businesses, especially those focused on traveling.

On the one hand, there are some positive points, like the cost effective communications, the closer relationship created with potential customers, it is also quick and easy for customers to get their travel products, and it encourages greater co-operations among traditional competitors (The Scottish Parliament, 2002). On the other hand, there are still many customers who prefer face to face contact, when requiring a specific service, or providing their private financial information.

The trend for future describes a slight growth despite the current economic recession. Moreover, in the next 10 years, one-third of travel buying population will get their travel products online, through specialized agencies, tour operators, airlines, and other similar organizations.

This kind of tourism provides more information to customers, and it gives them the possibility of being more interactive. For example, some tourism Web sites give the consumers the opportunity of rating the different activities or events showed in those Web sites, and they can also make suggestions to help other consumers when they are choosing a tourism destination.

STUDY OF THREE DIFFERENT WEB SITES

After analyzing the importance of the tourism sector in the different world economies and its repercussion for expanding the knowledge of new cultures, I have decided to study three different tourism Web sites to see whether they exceed customers' expectations.

The aim of this study is to see whether these Web sites are effective in promoting a concrete destination. I choose three different European countries to carry out this study.

The first country I chose was France, which in fact represents the most visited country by tourists, and it is in the fourth position in travel and tourism competitiveness. This destination offers both pleasant and romantic vacation and cultural tourism. The relaxing tourism is because of its coastlines, its "chateaux" and the city of Paris by itself. Couples like visiting these places because they feel involved by a romantic atmosphere. Furthermore, France offers adventure tourism, with its skiing resorts in the Alps, for all these people who like adventure and other similar sports.

I have also chosen Spain, which is the third most visited country after the United States, and it is in the sixth position in travel and tourism competitiveness. Spain has become a very important country in terms of tourism. Spain offers both cultural and pleasure vacation. In fact, a considerable number of people from the United Kingdom, Germany, and France visit its beautiful beaches of "La Costa Brava," "Marbella," and so on. However, this country also offers another type of places related to the cultural tourism, for instance, the cities of Seville, Granada, Santiago de Compostela, and so on.

In fact, Spain is the country with most World Heritage sites designated by UNESCO with 42 sites. Finally, I have to add that there has been observed a new trend over the past two years, which is the medical tourism due the excellent medical system that offers low cost and quality medical treatment for patients from all over the world. However, tourism rates have decreased over the past three years.

Portugal finishes with this study after the importance it has had over the past decade. Despite it is in the nineteenth position in international tourist arrivals and in the seventeenth position in travel and competitiveness, this country has had a substantial growth in terms of tourists, because of the attractiveness of its destinations.

This country gives the visitors the opportunity of having both cultural and pleasure tourism. On the one hand, there are a large number of monuments and cultural activities in its main cities such as Lisbon, Porto, or Sintra. On the other hand, this country offers tourists other kinds of distractions more related to leisure. For example, the islands of Madeira and Açores, the Algarve in the south of Portugal, and the beaches, which represent the west coast of Europe.

The reason for choosing these countries was to find out if their official Web sites were effective in promoting these places. As a result, the study is focused on France as the typical most visited destination, Spain as a growing tourist destination, and Portugal as an emerging tourist destination that has improved considerably its numbers over the past decade. Both France and Spain are in the world's top tourism destination. France is in the top position with 9.3% of market share in 2006, and Spain is in the second place with 6.9%.

METHOD

However, evaluating the success of these Web sites is difficult and quite subjective. That is why, this study measures the effectiveness of these sites in terms of the correspondence between what people want (the kind of tourism they are looking for) and what the Web site offers.

To carry out this analysis, the study examines in detail every official Web site, paying special attention to their content, visible effects, and other specific applications destined to make the Web sites more interactive and attractive to public. In other words, the study tries to test the effectiveness of these sites looking into some of their main elements, such as their number of languages, possible videos or sounds, website updates, practical information, partnerships, promotional materials, or the possibility of booking directly activities or events related to the tourism of these sites. After this in depth analysis, the study reaches a conclusion on which Web site is the best one in terms of effectiveness in promoting its destination.

France

This country has several Web sites where tourists can find reliable information about its most important destinations and the most remarkable events. This study focuses on the analysis of the official Web site of French tourism, http://www.franceguide.com.

Email traffic to Franceguide.com had had an increasing trend in 2009, and the traffic trend will likely be stable at this lever during 2010. In fact, the French Government Tourist Office owns this site, and the site provides visitors all the information they need to experience the perfect trip to France. Its home page contains important information in the top and bottom of the page, as well as in the center, and in the right, left side.

The top of the homepage has three sections: Press corner, Conventional Bureau, and Travel Trade. Furthermore, in the center of the homepage, there are some pictures in movement showing beautiful French places. Links are available to online media tools like *Facebook, Twitter, eNewsletter* (chats) and download applications (mobile phones). The center of the page has two more sections called "What's on now?" (tourist special sites, mountains in winter, and so on) and "Not to be missed" (that are special events and festivals). This section provides information about the different French regions and gives the consumers the opportunity of getting the magazine *Traveler in France* online or in a paper copy.

The tool bar contains the most important information of this Web site:

- Where to go:
  - A map of France and a list with the French regions, territories, and islands. When you click on them, you get some practical information about that region (tourist offices and tourism board information)
  - Research Book: last minute availabilities like hotels, villa rental, mobile home, and campsite pitch. If you click on them you can see the last offers and the location of the hotel in Google Maps
- What to do: activities and different kinds of holidays like naturism, mountains, shopping, cycling, villages, camping, culture, gay friendly, youth, and so on. When you click on them, you get some practical information and the possibility of acquiring its special brochure
- Brochures: all the brochures you can get on paper or downloaded
- Newsletters: latest newsletters bringing you up to date information on what's happening in the regions and some useful ideas for planning a trip to France. Furthermore, people can subscribe France guide. The French Tourist Board offers the opportunity to add to and manage a private account or personal space directly in Franceguide.com. Users can
  - Subscribe or unsubscribe to the French Tourist Bureau's eNewsletters
  - Check personal data
  - Participate in surveys

– WIN: competitions to get a chance of winning a trip to a specific region or some interesting products related to France guide
– Practical info: weather, getting married, entry requirements, motoring, transport, traveler's tips, and access to the guide of welcome France
– Affordable France: special activities, events, and so on that can be booked. Users can share their tips, rate, and make comments about these activities.

Finally, the right side of the homepage talks about the different French regions, the brochures (users can only order a maximum of six magazines), and a section called "Get organized," which contains useful information like weather.

In the bottom page, users can find different languages, vacancies, legal information, and advertising in France guide and a compilation of the main applications of this Web site.

Spain

The study is focused on the analysis of the official Web site of Spanish tourism, http://www.spain.info. In the top page, users can select their country (different languages), look for accommodation, book flight and rent a car, find practical Spanish information (culture, environments, society, geography, entry requirements, climate, politics, travel services, and so on), find information about TURESPAÑA Corporate Website (regarding the *Instituto de Turismo de España* and the work we carry out to promote Spanish tourism abroad), and a web map and the latest news. However, to access Newsletters, users have to be previously subscribed.

The tool bar has different interesting sections:

– Come:
  • About the main cities, possible destinations (Costa Brava, Pyrenees, and so on) and all the cities of Spain. If users click on that, they can see the main information about each place (culture, museums, events, a map, what to visit, where to sleep, and so on)
  • There is also a map to help their search
– Discover: Information about
  • Museums, Routes, Monuments, historic gardens, and World Heritage sites. If users click on them, they can see practical information. Users cannot book any activities or events
  • Calendar of the next events, for booking them users have to go to the official website event

– Enjoy: Activities – sports, having fun, nature, the sea, and so on. Users cannot book them
– Taste:
  • Spanish cuisine: recipes
  • Spanish wines: routes
  • Cuisine events
  • Possibility of finding a specific restaurant, but without the booking option
– Experience: it talks about
  • Festivities events
  • Culture events
  • Sports events
  • Conference events

Finally, in the center of the page there are the main events/activities, and in the bottom page users can find some legal information and reserve accommodation online.

Portugal

The main information about Portuguese tourism comes from its official tourism Web site, http://www.visitportugal.com.

Its top page only shows beautiful images of Portugal, and users can choose among the nine different languages. In the center of the page, users can find resources (restaurants, hotels, and so on), see the main events that cannot be booked, and explore Portugal with the aid of an interactive map. Furthermore, in the bottom page, users can find legal information and log in to their account. They have the possibility of get registered in order to have access to the latest news.

The tool bar has different sections:

– Experience: different kinds of activities/holidays. For example, relax, golf, arts, adventure, romance, and so on. If users click on that, they get a list with the main places related to that activity with practical info. Moreover, people can rate and make their own suggestions, but without the possibility of booking them
– Destinations: the main touristic regions of Portugal. A list with the most beautiful places from there, and information about where to eat, where to stay, events, and so on. Users cannot book them

– About Portugal: accommodation, climate, driving, cost of living, history, transports, and so on. No booking, just information
– Getting here: it says how users can get to Portugal from the place they are (train, plane, and so on). However, they cannot book anything
– My holiday plan: users can create their itinerary
– Find: search any kind of information.

Finally, the left side of the homepage shows information about the latest promotions and events, and it has a multimedia section:

– Facebook and Twitter
– Maps: users can download different maps in large or small version
– Videos: users can download or play videos from Portugal
– Podcasts: users have to be subscripted to Really Simple Syndication (RSS)
– Brochures: free brochures that can be downloaded
– Postcards: beautiful postcard that can be sent to friends.

CONCLUSIONS

Fesenmaier and Kim (2008) consider different hypothesis when measuring the effectiveness of a destination Web site, for example, in terms of the quantity of information, usability, credibility, inspiration, and reciprocity with consumers. As commented before, this study examines the effectiveness of these sites depending on how well these Web sites respond to customers' needs about tourism. As a result, the most important factors here are the quantity and quality of information (Diaz, Esteban, & Martin-Consuegra, 2009), as well as the ability of the web page for being inspirational and reciprocal (through multimedia and social effects).

The three Web sites provide very useful information about their destinations. However, they offer different kinds of applications. This study considered different questions related to the Web site applications to see whether the website is useful to the customer. The key points of these questions are listed in Table 1.

Table 1 shows strengths and weakness of these websites in terms of their applications. On the one hand, France guide is the Web site that offers more applications and accessibility to users. On the other hand, VisitPortugal is the most innovating and interactive Web site because of its videos and multimedia applications. On the contrary, the official Web site of

Table 1. Web Sites Applications.

Website	France	Spain	Portugal
Languages	>20	>15	9
Videos	No	No	Yes
Sounds	No	No	Yes
Images	Images in movement	Pictures of celebrities and special events	Images of the west coast
Brochures or guides	Yes (online and paper copy)	No	Yes (online and paper copy)
Booking	Yes	No	No
Colors	Very colored pages (pink, orange, blue, yellow,...)	It plays with the colors of its flag over a black background	Light colors over a white background
Social media	Yes	No	Yes
Information	Yes	Yes	Yes
Maps	Yes	Yes	Yes
Membership	Yes	Users have to be registered to get the latest news	Yes

Table 2. Advantages and Disadvantages of Each Web Site.

	Advantages	Disadvantages
France Guide	– It offers a huge quantity of useful information – Possibility of booking activities and events directly from this website	– The text is poor structured and it results confusion for users – No multimedia effects – No history of France
Spain.info	– Very structured and cohesive website – It provides interesting information about the Spanish history, cuisine,... – Easy to manage	– No multimedia effects – No booking options – No magazines
Visitportugal	– Multimedia effects and sounds – Memberships	– Poor quantity of information limited only to the main Portuguese destinations – No booking possibilities

tourism from Spain gives less opportunities of interaction with users, and its applications are more limited.

To finish with the analysis, the study examines carefully the advantages and disadvantages of each Web site.

Table 2 shows that the French website is the one that provides more useful information to users, despite its lack on multimedia effects. The

Portuguese website is innovative in terms of applications, but it is really behind in the quantity of information provided. Finally, the Spanish Web site is easy to manage and results are eye-catching, but it does not give any other facilities to users.

After this in-depth analysis, and considering the aforementioned factors when evaluating the Web sites effectiveness, it is clear that France wide is the most successful tourism Web site in promoting the French destinations. However, a good challenge for this Web site would be introducing more innovating and multimedia effects in the homepage to attract the attention of users.

ACKNOWLEDGMENTS

The author acknowledges the helpful comments of two anonymous Boston College colleagues. She is responsible for all limitations and errors that may relate to the study.

REFERENCES

Bowen, T. J., Kotler, P., & Makens, C. J. (2010). *Marketing for hospitality and tourism* (5th ed.). New Jersey, NY: Pearson.

Diaz, E., Esteban, A., & Martin-Consuegra, D. (2009). Evaluación de la eficacia de las páginas web: un análisis de contenido de las principales compañías aéreas. Dialnet, OAI Articles, pp. 279–293.

Fesenmaier, R. D., & Kim, H. (2008). Persuasive design of destination web sites: An analysis of first impression. *Journal of Travel Research, 47*(3), 3–13.

The Scottish Parliament. (2002). *Tourism E-Business.* The information Centre, 02/93.

Tourism Marketing on the Internet. Available at http://www.netstarter.com.au/Content_Common/pg-internet-tourism-marketing.seo

USEFULNESS OF GOVERNMENT AND PRIVATE DESTINATION WEBSITES

Christopher P. Dion and Arch G. Woodside

ABSTRACT

American tourism is largely affected by the ability and ease with which one can travel to a tourist destination. Information availability, utility, and value of information on websites are essential in choosing and planning a vacation or business trip. This study compares visa and nonvisa tourist destinations as they relate to American tourism and business travel. Each destination's internet website quality, quantity, and utility are compared through an evaluation rubric with 36 attributes. Four countries are considered to provide two countries in each category of visa required and nonvisa required. The marketing mediums compared are the government run websites and Lonely Planet's private sector version. The first proposition is that countries that require visas lack the quality and quantity in internet marketing in comparison to those countries that do not require a visa. The second proposition is that the government run websites are comprehensive in detailing information in comparison to privately created websites. The eight complete rubrics achieve a comparison that is comprehensive demonstrating variability in quality and information available. The third proposition addresses is the fact

Tourism-Marketing Performance Metrics and Usefulness Auditing of Destination Websites
Advances in Culture, Tourism and Hospitality Research, Volume 4, 69–137
ISSN: 1871-3173/doi:10.1108/S1871-3173(2010)0000004010

that the quality of the government run websites relates strongly to the overall web presence and periodical existence of that particular countries' tourist destination literature. This chapter is unique and valuable to those considering travel to a visa-required destination but the theories demonstrated highlight the deficiencies of private sector websites and the fast pace growth of internet tourism marketing.

INTRODUCTION

The visa requirements for Americans traveling abroad can be intimidating, confusing, and foreboding when choosing a foreign tourist destination. Governments of foreign countries have a revenue and social interest to promote positive tourism aspects as well as to outline and explain visa requirements. The internet has become the primary means by which destination marketing organizations (DMOs) communicate with prospective tourists (Kim & Fesenmaier, 2010). There exists a vast difference in quality and quantity of information available when comparing government run tourism marketing websites and those of the private sector.

This study compares the internet marketing of countries that require a visa in comparison to those that do not. The study also compares the quality, utility, and value of government DMO tourism websites to websites created and managed by a private firm. Lonely Planet websites were chosen as the private sector comparison group for consistency, foreign presence, and availability. The countries chosen not only to compare and share similar visa requirements for American tourists and business people but also represent geographic, economic, and social similarities as well: Russia, Poland, China, and Thailand. Although previous web-based studies compare persuasive design, first impression or utility, no articles compare the barriers to marketing that visa requirements can make. Further, quantitative assessments comparing government DMO marketing and private sector websites provide insights to both organizations' successes and failures.

The Lonely Planet marketing websites pale in comparison to the individual countries proprietary DMO's version. These differences are highlighted by the attributes detailed in the completed rubrics for the various websites and countries. Review completed rubrics in the appendix to learn the evaluations of each website. This study uses the Woodside and Dion (2010) rubric for evaluating DMO websites. The strength of the Lonely Planet website is that it encourages the traveler to purchase its literature, thereby earning profits selling travel books. The lack of current information, explicit detail and valuable travel insight, however, is significantly deficient in the private sector when compared to the government run websites. The government DMOs achieving virtual complete success of the rubric attributes is somewhat alarming to those who may doubt the ability of government DMOs to provide internet-based services.

The number of periodicals available relates substantially to the number of texts available when comparing individual countries. The overall web presence of each country also correlates perfectly to the amount of tourism texts and periodicals available. Finally, the quality of each countries government run website does not correlate to the two aforementioned variables. Three of the four government run websites for both visa and nonvisa required countries were outstanding in achieving most the 36 attributes of the rubric regardless of other comparative factors. The government websites' DMOs deserve recognition for providing better quality and improved quantity of information in comparison to the private sector company.

The objectives of this study include: (1) comparing visa and nonvisa required tourist destination websites as two entities, qualitatively identify and discuss visa section; (2) compare government DMO websites and private sector website using rubric attributes; (3) highlight individual countries' internet tourism marketing presence, tourism marketing text presence, periodical tourism presence in the context of each varying websites utility and value; and (4) discuss the reprehensible lack of available information for handicapped and physically disabled tourists in all internet marketing mediums.

Additional research is necessary in defining variables in quality, utility, and value of private sector websites in visa and nonvisa required destinations. The private sector website Lonely Planet used in research does not allow you to apply directly for a visa. Regardless of direct applicability, the visa requirements of Russia alone could preclude it from being a tourist destination. The websites provide ample information outlining the visa application process, however, the visa itself may be a tourist deterrent. The quality of all government DMOs internet marketing may outweigh the inconvenience for a few savvy travelers. With the exception of Russia, China, Poland, and Thailand all have brilliant government DMO marketing sites to guide you including user reviews and blogs which educate the intricacies of foreign travel.

VISA VERSUS NONVISA REQUIRED DESTINATIONS: THE TRAVELING AMERICAN'S DILEMMA

The world's tourism industry is dynamically changing with free travel restricted only by fears of terrorism and personal finance. Countries that were previously inaccessible to Americans like Russia and China now welcome tourists while maintaining visa requirements. The information available to tourists and business people has also made traveling more accessible by providing useful and valuable information via the Internet. Authors and readers alike have been transformed by "blogging," recounting their experiences and lessons learned. Despite the relative success of government DMO and private sector marketing efforts of visa requirements the visa itself may preclude the destination for tourists.

The information available on the internet continues to grow each day. There is a wealth of information in today's internet age compared to when travel research was conducted in the library alone. Table 1 highlights the disparity of information available when conducting tourism research on Russia, China, Thailand, and Poland on-line versus the library. Table 1 also highlights the near perfect correlation of on-line resources to text and periodicals available.

The wealth of information available on the internet takes away most of the mystery about the visa requirements of countries. In comparing visa and nonvisa required tourist destinations through eight rubrics, the visa requirement was easily identifiable in all sites. The visa requirements of Russia, however, may impede visiting the country. Despite both Russia's government DMO website and the Lonely Planet Russia website do a great job in describing the visa requirement and process the visa itself is restrictive. The lack of flexibility in Russia's visa requirements and expense make of the visa are deterrents regardless of how clearly defined and well explained the visa may be.

Table 1. Available Websites and Boston College Books on Countries.

Country	"[Country] Tourism" (000)	"[Country]" (000)	BC Library Texts "[County] Tourism"
China	58,100	568,000	23
Thailand	30,200	173,000	4
Russia	11,000	169,000	4
Poland	13,400	157,000	0

All of the government DMO internet tourist websites averaged collectively 32 of the 36 attributes on the rubric. Russia was the weak link, however, as an individual country and brings the average down. The private sector (Lonely Planet) averaged 23 of the 36 attributes. The appendix includes seethe-specific findings for the rubric applications for reference.

The fact that a country has a visa requirement (Russia and China) has no impact on the quality of the site although Russia in general lacks substantial amounts of information. Visa required countries, especially a populous country like China and an economically poor one like Russia, still have great quality websites despite previously not welcoming tourists. The poor quality, utility, and quantity of information from Russia necessitates further research as to whether or not visa required countries are less focused on tourism. Additional countries that fail to achieve the attributes of the rubric would substantiate a hypothesis that countries requiring visas are less tourist-friendly. The variations between visa required and nonvisa required tourist destinations (Russia's poor websites) was virtually offset by China (visa required) which quantitatively and qualitatively provided the best website.

The visa process is distinctly superior on government DMO websites in comparison with the private sector Lonely Planet website. Russia and China allow individuals both to apply directly for the visa on the site and both websites do a better job of detailing the different types of visas.

Each country's website provide more details that the Lonely Planet site. The private sector website does do a "fine" job out describing the visa process but the ability to interact with the countries' consulate and embassy is amazing. A tourist traveling to a visa required country should visit the country's government DMO website. Lonely Planet's smart and witty writing cannot surpass the visa required countries' DMO in communication, organization, and ease. Fig. 1 outlines the simplified process the visa has become in the age of technology and the internet.

GOVERNMENT DMO WEBSITES IN COMPARISON TO PRIVATE SECTOR WEBSITES

Lonely Planet fails in comparison with government DMO tourism websites. The private sector's failure is not surprising, however, given the decrease of

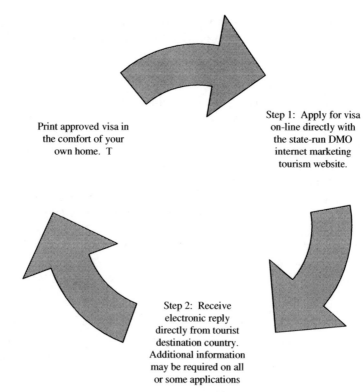

Print approved visa in
the comfort of your
own home. T

Step 1: Apply for visa
on-line directly with
the state-run DMO
internet marketing
tourism website.

Step 2: Receive
electronic reply
directly from tourist
destination country.
Additional information
may be required on all
or some applications

Fig. 1. Electronic Visa Application Process with Government DMO Tourism
Websites.

tourist books and accordingly the publishing business. According to AAP
Yearly Industry reporting the sales of books in 2009 was down by 1.8%.
One hypothesizes is that the reduction in sales does not allow the private
sector organization to maintain funding for current writing and updating of
the websites. The government DMO websites were robust in information
and content. The number of videos between the two entities (Government
DMO and Private sector) was not comparable as China's DMO website
hosted approximately 90 videos in comparison to Lonely Planet's 12 videos.

Quantitatively the attribute rubric ratings distinguish the DMOs websites
in comparison to Lonely Planet's sites. Regardless of whether or not the
country requires a visa, the government DMO websites were superior
in utility and value. A common factor among all websites was the lack
of information the varying organizations were willing to mail free literature.

The exception to this criterion was Poland's government website which provides ample tourist information on specific topics, maps, and posters.

The underlying motive of Lonely Planet is for the tourist to purchase their guidebook. E-newsletter updates, information, and resources were all free in the government sponsored sites. Again, Poland government sponsored site offers to mail an abundance of marketing materials. The move to mail less tangible items (one classmate described receiving a coupon book from a State that was expired) is a deliberate move by DMOs to reduce costs and is a product of the internet. Digital media can be transmitted for free and more rapidly accessible. Poland's willingness to mail material fits their hospitable mantra of welcoming tourists and being known as particularly friendly and accommodating to visitors. With respect to this Polish distinction, every question included in the rubric was answered positively among all eight evaluations.

Tables 2 and 3 provide comparisons of the Lonely Planet and government DMO websites.

China is consistently the best represented country in both marketing media. Another constant within the comparison of website marketing mediums is the superior quality of the government DMO websites. The government DMOs present more expansive and detailed information overall. The ease of use for all of the government DMO sites ranged from outstanding to good. Conversely, the ease of use for the private sector website Lonely Planet was only moderate for all four countries.

The Russian government DMO website was the only exception of a private sector website (Lonely Planet) being better than the government DMO site: in Table 2, the Lonely Planet site scores 10 versus the DMO site scoring 5. The lack of quality and information on the Russia DMO site may suggest that the Russian government is not as focused on tourism as other countries. Because Russia is a visa-required destination it may be indicative of all visa-required countries having less quality sites. Interestingly, on the Lonely Planet websites Russia scores higher than the other countries due to the fact that Russia was differentiated by current events and attractions in June.

The Chinese government DMO website has the most languages available (10) and the best safety and security information. The Lonely Planet website had seven languages available in all country sites. Russia's DMO site only had 5 languages available which was the lowest of all websites compared. Thailand's government DMO site had the best interactive games of sites compared whereas the private sector sites did not offer the interactive game function. Poland's private sector website had the best historical information

Table 2. Findings Using Woodside/Dion Rubric for Each Country Using Lonely Planet Website.

Attribute	China	Russia	Thailand	Poland
Hotel booking	Yes, link provided	Yes, link provided	Yes, link Provided	Yes
Hotel amenities- 4+	Yes	Yes	Yes	Yes
Event booking	No	No	No	No
Membership	Yes, membership is free	Yes, membership	Yes	Yes
Brochures in mail	No	No	No	No
Attractions in June	No	Yes	No	No
Ease of use	Moderate	Moderate	Moderate	Moderate
Current events calendar	No	List only. No calendar	No	No
Videos	Yes, great travel videos	Yes	Yes	Yes
Maps	Yes, country map	Yes	Yes	Yes
Cell phone apps	No	No	No	No
Historical information	Yes, very complete	Yes	Yes	Yes detailed/ Poetic
Visa information	Yes	Yes	Yes	Yes
Family information	*No*	No	No	No
Disabilities	No	No	No	No
Interactive games	No	No	No	No
Languages	7 Total languages!	7 Total languages	7 Total languages	7 Languages
Safety security	Yes, detailed	Yes, detailed	Yes, detailed	Yes
Totals	10	12	10	10

(detailed and poetic) despite all eight sites analyzed having the inclusion of historical information.

The comparison tables all indicate that the government DMO websites are doing a better job than the private sector with the exception of Russia. Reviewing the details in the Appendix for the individual items in the evaluation rubric for each destination website supports the summary findings in Tables 2 and 3.

INTERNET MARKETING SUCCESS – POLAND DEFIES ODDS WHILE CHINA MEETS EXPECTATIONS

China has the largest web presence out of the four countries in this study. On 4/29/10, "China Tourism" was entered into the Google internet search

Table 3.   Findings Using Woodside/Dion Rubric for DMO (State)
Run Website.

Attribute	China	Russia	Thailand	Poland
Hotel booking	Yes	Yes	Yes	Yes
Hotel amenities – 4+	Yes	Yes	Yes	Yes
Event booking	No	No	No	No
Membership	Yes	No	Yes	No
Brochures in mail	No	No	No	Yes
Attractions in June	Yes	No	Yes	Yes
Ease of Use	Outstanding	Moderate	Good	Good
Current Events Calendar	Yes	No	Yes	Yes
Videos	Yes	No	Yes	Yes
Maps	Yes	No	Yes	Yes
Cell Phone Apps	Yes	No	No	No
Historical Information	Yes	No	Yes	Yes
Visa Information	Yes	Yes	Yes	Yes
Family Information	*Yes*	No	Yes	Yes
Disabilities	No	No	No	No
Interactive Games	Yes	No	Yes- The Best	No
Languages	Yes, 10!	Yes, only 2	Yes, only 2	Yes, 11
Safety and Security	Yes- Detailed	No	Yes	Yes
Totals	15	5	14	13

engine resulting in 58.1 million internet options. China also had the best
government sponsored website of the four countries compared in regard to
utility, value, and content. An interesting topic for future research would be
to study if a countries' population size correlates to their overall marketing
presence and quality. China is also a visa required country and is at the
opposite end of the spectrum in overall quality compared to the other visa
required country Russia.

Future research using the attributes of the rubric on a visa required
country could confirm the hypothesis that visa required countries need
improvements in their government DMO marketing sites in general. China
would be the exception to do the success in current DMO marketing efforts.
Finally, from the overall quality of a visa required DMO website China have
less interest than other countries in tourism and certainly does not rely on
tourism for revenue.

All government DMO websites were interesting, engaging, and informative in one way or another. Russia again contributes the least information
as an individual country. From interactive Thai massages to virtual water
rafting race, the research for the study was fun and captivating.

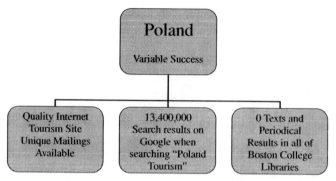

Fig. 2.   Poland's Unique Value Proposition.

A particular stand out for overall quality was Poland. A nonvisa required country Poland is particularly attractive to the American tourist. Prices are inexpensive while at the same time history and activities abound. The website's quality is remarkable given the website presence of only 13,400,000 resulted when "Poland Tourism" is googled. The success of Poland as a DMO is profound as they lack web presence but also text and periodical presence. Fig. 2 is the three components of Poland's marketing using the comparable aspects of the study.

MARKET MEDIUMS FAIL TO ADDRESS HANDICAP AND DISABLED TOURISM

All eight rubric evaluations highlight a shared marketing failure: handicap accessibility in the four tourist destinations. The failure of all websites, government DMO and private sector, visa and nonvisa required countries demonstrates the need for awareness for those travelers with disabilities within our marketing and tourism industry. Question number 27 of the rubric is the one attribute which some would consider the most pertinent questions: Is there information available for people with physical disabilities or handicaps? Without the answer to the question, "Can I physically navigate this tourist destination if I can not walk?" sadly may not be able to take part. Public transportation, sidewalk accessibility and a litany of critical details have become prevalent in American society. As an American tourist we are unfortunately not provided with these pertinent details when traveling to the four studied countries.

Question 27 of the rubric might be the distinguishing factor between a website's excellence or lack thereof. I encourage all researchers to use this metric in evaluating and quantifying a website's content. As mentioned, the American Disabilities Act changed tourism and marketing in America which in turn changed a culture. Foreign destinations will hopefully progress in this regard as they have in internet marketing and creating such effective DMOs.

REFLECTIONS AND CONCLUSION

The rubrics themselves could be a travel guide or at a minimum a guide in choosing a travel destination and attaining a visa. The research for the project was vast and enjoyable. Accordingly, there is work still to be done in comparing visa and nonvisa required tourist destinations. The end result is that the DMOs of government destinations are doing a great job in marketing their countries in comparison with the private sector. The act of having to apply for visa and incur additional costs for visa is a tourism barrier in itself. All marketing mediums did a great job of detailing visa requirements and the processes as evidenced by the four rubrics on this specific subject. I surmise some private sector companies are doing a better job then Lonely Planet as well. Russia's government DMO and private sector websites were low in utility, quality, and value in comparison to China, Thailand, and Poland. Additional research is needed to identify a trend of poor marketing in visa required countries.

The lack of information available in all marketing mediums for tourist with physical disabilities is disheartening. The group forums on all sites provided recommendations and real-life insight to navigating all of the studied tourist destinations. A universal recommendation to all marketing medium creators, DMOs, and tourism and marketing research analysts is to include access to people with physical disabilities. A further recommendation would be to promote and highlight blogs and group forums, similar to those featured in China's government DMO site. After conducting the initial research the study turned to looking for the quality of blogs and group forums. Another disparity juxtaposes style and content. The often well-written information displayed on the Lonely Planet sites endears itself to the American tourist and is not fully captured by foreign DMOs, yet the foreign DMOs' exhaustive list of relevant, current, and well-organized information dwarfs Lonely Planet as the overall best tourism representation.

ACKNOWLEDGMENT

The authors acknowledge the creative input and editing of Sheri Dion to this chapter. Sheri Dion is an inspiration to Chris Dion not only in his pursuit and interest in travel but also in life. The authors acknowledge Emile J Dion, III for his editing of the chapter. Finally, the authors acknowledge Lauren Fryc for the addition of the website comparison tables while editing the chapter.

REFERENCES

Kim, H., & Fesenmaier, D. R. (2010). Persuasive design of destination websites: An analysis of first impression. *Journal of Travel Research*, *47*(1), 3–13.

Woodside, A., & Dion, C. P. (2010). *Website customer usefulness rubric*. Working Paper. Boston College, Carroll School of Management, Department of Marketing, Chestnut Hill, MA.

Websites:

china.org.cn
TourismThailand.org
http://www.lonelyplanet.com/china
http://www.lonelyplanet.com/poland
http://www.lonelyplanet.com/russia
http://www.lonelyplanet.com/thailand
http://www.poland.travel/en/
http://www.visitrussia.org.uk/

APPENDIX. ANALYSIS OF DESTINATION MARKETING WEBSITES USING THE WOODSIDE & DION RUBRIC CHINA GOVERNMENT SPONSORED RUBRIC

Researcher's Name: Christopher P. Dion
Date: 4/05/2010

Website brand: Government-sponsored
Website address: china.org.cn

Ed note: I love this site! It made me want us to visit China. It had so much information and was much more detailed and relevant than the Lonely Planet site. Awesome weather!! Great current events, activities, top things to see, tons more info on the forum, and "learn Chinese" was interactive and perfect. You can also download info on your mobile device or PDA at: m.china.org.cn.

Issues:

Can I book a moderately priced hotel room at this website for a 10-day visit in mid-June 2010? ($150 per night)

Minutes searching for answer: Yes (x)   No ()   Not sure ()

Comments: Many hotels available, 5 star hotels for $90!!!

What do I get for this hotel room (free internet? Use of exercise room? Swimming pool?)

Minutes searching: 1   Not sure ()   1–3 amenities ()   4+ amenities (x)

Comments:

Souvenir/Gift Shop(s)	Business Facilities	Elevator Lift
Conference Facilities	Currency Exchange	Doctor on Call
Bank	Laundry/Valet	Bar
Disabled Facilities	Massage	Sauna
Gym	Swimming Pool Indoor	Tennis
Solarium	Swimming Pool	

3. Does the official site tell me what special events are available in mid-June 2010?

Minutes searching for answer: 6   Yes (x)   No ()   Not sure ()

Comments: See Events and Festivals.

4. If yes, can I book one of these events on-line at the official website?

Minutes searching: 2   Yes ()   No (x)   Not sure ()

Comments: (Describe events)

Vegetable Fair attracts visitors	May 4
Bird show held in SW China's Guilin	May 4
Kunming Tourism Festival kicks off in SW China	May 4
E-Mart to open first shopping mall in Shanghai	April 30
"I swear a low-carbon living" living	April 29
5th Int'l Birds Viewing Festival opens at China-DPRK border city	April 29
Ship parade to mark opening of Suzhou Int'l Tourism Festival	April 27
Art-will travel to Yi House	April 27
More trains for Yangtze Delta's needs	April 26
Tourism drying up	April 26

5. Can I become a "member" at this website? (If yes, do become a member if membership if free.)

Minutes searching: 2   Yes (x)   No ()   Not sure ()

Comments: Yes.

6. Can I pay to become a special member (e.g., pay dues) at this website?

Minutes searching: Yes ()   No (x)   Not sure ()

Comments:

Registration provides free and instant access to China Wiki, China Answers, City Guide, Forum and more on China.org.cn.

7. What do I get for membership at the website?

Minutes searching: 2   Multiple perks (x)   No ()   Not sure ()

Comments: See comments 6.

8. Does the website tell me what unique "must do" attractions that I should visit in June?

Minutes searching: 4   Yes (x)   No ()   Not sure ()

Comments:

9. Can I book one of these attractions at the official website?

Minutes searching: 2   Yes ()   No (x)   Not sure ()

Comments: The website links to tourism/travel agencies.

10. Does the website offer free paper copy literature that will be mailed to me?

Minutes searching: 4   Yes ()   No (x)   Not sure ()

Comments: You can sign up for an on-line newsletter, mobile news, RSS feeds.

If yes, request this literature and record the date of the request and when you receive the literature. N/A.

11. Are videos shown at this website?

Minutes searching: 5   Yes (x)   No ()   Not sure ()

Comments: There are multiple travel videos. Better than Lonely planet – MUCH better organized.

12. If yes, can I select a video that shows visitors doing things that I prefer to do at this destination?

Minutes searching: 10   Yes (x)   No ()   Not sure ()

Comments: Example: 563,000 visitors tour Expo Park in first 3 days, picturesque scenery in China's Guangxi.

13. Can I see a map of the destination at the website?

Minutes searching: 2   Yes (x)   No ()   Not sure ()

Comments: On main page – also links for city maps.

Can I request a map be sent to me via mail from this website?

Minutes searching: 4   Yes ()   No (x)   Not sure ()

Comments: China.org.cn has just launched its mobile version, offering the latest news from China and around the world.

To get access, just log onto m.china.org.cn with your mobile phone, PDA or other mobile device.

China.org.cn mobile consists of 11 sections, covering the latest in business, political, sports, and entertainment events. You can also get daily bilingual news, as well as travel information and tips.

For easier access, you can bookmark the link or save it as a favorite on your mobile phone.

Data charges may apply, please consult your mobile service providers.

16. Can I book a classical upscale restaurant at the official website?

Minutes searching: 5   Yes ( )   No (x)   Not sure ( )

Comments: Link to travel agencies. Tours Suppliers:

Top China Tours   China CTS tours   China Travel   China Tour   Travel to China

Minutes to book: N/A   Easy to do ( )   Hard to do ( )   Not sure ( )

Comments: N/A.

18. Does the website offer information for visits by families with young children?

Minutes searching: 4   Yes (x)   No ( )   Not sure ( )

Comments: Tons and tons of activities are listed. Themed Tours

Adventure	Great Wall
Bicycling	Hiking & Trekking
Birds Watching	Hunting
Canoeing	Language Schools
Caving	Martial Arts
Cruise	Mountain Climbing
Culture Journey	Photography
Eco Tourism	Railway Trips
Farm Stay	Scuba Diving
Fishing	Spiritual Vacations
Food & Wine	Wildlife Viewing
Golf	

19. Can the visitor to the website ask for a mailing of literature about visiting for a family of two adults and two children 4 and 9 years old?

Minutes searching: 4   Yes ( )   No (x)   Not sure ( )

Comments: You can receive info on mobile device.

20. Does the website offer an interactive game to play?

Minutes searching: 2   Yes (x)   No ( )   Not sure ( )

Comments: While not a game per say, you can learn survival Chinese and other fun Chinese phrases. It's free and has over 60 lessons. Better than the Rosetta Stone Chinese we have at home!

If yes, does the game provide further information about the destination and trip procedures to follow in visiting the destination?

Minutes searching: No, but the forum Q/A does.

21. Can you find a photograph of a visitor at this website that looks like you?

Minutes searching: 4   Yes (x)   No ()   Not sure ()

Comments: If "looks like me" equivocates to "American," yes.

22. Can you information about what to do in case of a health or police emergency at this website?

Minutes searching: 4   Yes (x)   No ()   Not sure ()

Comments:

23. Does the website include specific information about shopping and specific stores to buy luxury goods?

Minutes searching: 5   Yes (x)   No ()   Not sure ()

Comments: Detailed in what to do, slideshows, etc.

24. Does the website allow buying of specific products offered by specific stores via this official website?

Minutes searching: 5   Yes ()   No (x)   Not sure ()

Comments: Links at the bottom to wholesale clothes and stores.

25. Does the website tell about the night clubs and night life?

Minutes searching: 5   Yes (x)   No ()   Not sure ()

Comments:

26. Does the website permit booking to specific night clubs and night life events?

Minutes searching: 4   Yes ()   No (x)   Not sure ()

Comments: Travel agencies.

27. Does this website provide information for handicapped, impaired, visitors/customers/students?

Minutes searching: 5   Yes ()   No (x)   Not sure ()

Comments: No.

28. Is there a calendar of openings, holidays, closings, and/or special events at this website?

Minutes searching: 10   Yes (x)   No ()   Not sure ()

Comments: Events are listed in terms of articles.

29. Is current weather available as well as weather by month of year at this website?

Minutes searching: 12   Yes, current weather (x)   Yes, for all months (x)

No current weather ()   No weather for each month ()   Not sure ()

Comments: Fantastic weather feature, including an area/city map.

30. Is the website available in languages other than English?

Minutes searching: 15 s   Yes (x)   No ()   Not sure ()

31. If yes, list all languages available at website:

English, Dutch, French, Russian, Spanish, Chinese, Japanese, Esperanto (!!!!), BIG5, Korean

Comments: This is portrayed at the top of the site.

32. Is historical information available at website?

Minutes searching: 1   Yes ()   No (x)   Not sure ()

Comments: This is a more current events site. If you subscribe, you can see the Archives ... but it's not like Lonely Planet where you get pages of specific history.

33. Is one or more slideshows of still photographs shown at the website?

Minutes searching: 4   Yes (x)   No ()   Not sure ()

Comments: Tons and tons and tons of HD photos.

34. Is one or more videos shown at the website?

Minutes searching: 1   Yes (x)   No ()   Not sure ()   If yes, how many videos?

Comments: Again, tons of information and well-organized.

35. Is safety/security information given at the website?

Minutes searching: 2   Yes (x)   No ()   Not sure ()

Comments: It's much more general information, but contains some great links. The Forum (needs more moderators) – also contains security/safety topics. It's a very advanced forum!

36. Does this website give visa requirements information?

Yes (x)

Comments:

Visa issue – Forum, China.org has relevant information about both tourism and travel visas.

China Private Sector Rubric

Researcher's Name: Christopher P. Dion
Date: 4/05/2010

Website brand: Lonely Planet (Global)

Website address: http://www.lonelyplanet.com/china

Issues: (aside) I love the introduction (again the lonely planet writers do not disappoint: "the most populous, most culturally idiosyncratic nation on earth."

Can I book a moderately priced hotel room at this website for a 10-day visit in mid-June 2010? ($150 per night)

Minutes searching for answer: 4   Yes (x)   No ()   Not sure ()

Comments: Many options were under 150. I picked a 4-star hotel for $88.

What do I get for this hotel room (free internet?; use of exercise room?; swimming pool?)

Minutes searching: 1   Not sure ()   1–3 amenities ()   4+ amenities (x)

Comments: (Park Plaza Beijing) Gym, beauty salon, massage center, internet, bar, restaurant, babysitting services, and business center.

3. Does the official site tell me what special events are available in mid-June 2010?

Minutes searching for answer: 6   Yes ( )   No (x)   Not sure ( )

Comments: It mentions June through October as the best time frame to visit. Under "tips and articles" it mentions best things to do in March, but not June.

4. If yes, can I book one of these events on-line at the official website?

Minutes searching: 2   Yes ( )   No (x)   Not sure ( )

Comments: (Describe events) N/A.

5. Can I become a "member" at this website? (If yes, do become a member if membership if free.)

Minutes searching: 2   Yes (x)   No ( )   Not sure ( )

Comments: It's free to be a member.

6. Can I pay to become a special member (e.g., pay dues) at this website?

Minutes searching: Yes ( )   No (x)   Not sure ( )

Comments: It seems as though this is a free site.

7. What do I get for membership at the website?

Minutes searching: 2   Multiple perks (x)   No ( )   Not sure ( )

Comments: Get and share tips, find groups to travel with, save trip places and itineraries, rate and review places you've been.

8. Does the website tell me what unique "must do" attractions that I should visit in June?

Minutes searching: 4   Yes ( )   No (x)   Not sure ( )

Comments: Again it mentions June as being one of the best months to visit.

9. Can I book one of these attractions at the official website?

Minutes searching: 2   Yes ( )   No (x)   Not sure ( )

Comments: The website links to other websites.

10. Does the website offer free paper copy literature that will be mailed to me?

Minutes searching: 4   Yes ( )   No (x)   Not sure ( )

Comments: Travel guides can be purchased. You can sign up for an on-line newsletter as well.

If yes, request this literature and record the date of the request and when you receive the literature. N/A

11. Are videos shown at this website?

Minutes searching: 5   Yes (x)   No ()   Not sure ()

Comments: There are multiple travel videos.

12. If yes, can I select a video that shows visitors doing things that I prefer to do at this destination?

Minutes searching: 10   Yes (x)   No ()   Not sure ()

Comments: "The Dammed Yangtze" – river boat cruise, the Beijing guide to lonely planet (bicycles, technology, the Forbidden City, Tiananmen Square, southern neighborhoods behind auto-routes, where you can still see no electricity, no running water, people talking about where they are moving, the Olympics (outdated reference), it's a perfect city for bike riding, karaoke bars, pub crawls/bars), a video on Macau's dwarfing Las Vegas in gambling/ casino monoculture, and snow in Shanghai. Great videos!

13. Can I see a map of the destination at the website?

Minutes searching: 2   Yes (x)   No ()   Not sure ()

Comments: Click on "show map."

Can I request a map be sent to me via mail from this website?

Minutes searching: 4   Yes ()   No (x)   Not sure ()

Comments: You have to buy literature on this website.

16. Can I book a classical upscale restaurant at the official website?

Minutes searching: 5   Yes ()   No (x)   Not sure ()

Comments: A table cannot be reserved here. Under "tips and articles" there is an article entitled, "Should China ban dog meat?" (10 MAR 2010) I/we could never even THINK about ingesting what the Chinese consider, according to this article, "a longstanding culinary tradition."

Minutes to book: N/A   Easy to do ()   Hard to do ()   Not sure ()

Comments: N/A.

18. Does the website offer information for visits by families with young children?

Minutes searching: 4   Yes ()   No (x)   Not sure ()

Comments: No mention of activities for families.

19. Can the visitor to the website ask for a mailing of literature about visiting for a family of two adults and two children 4 and 9 years old?

Minutes searching: 4   Yes ()   No (x)   Not sure ()

Comments: This website does not mail literature for free.

20. Does the website offer an interactive game to play?

Minutes searching: 2   Yes ()   No (x)   Not sure ()

Comments:

If yes, does the game provide further information about the destination and trip procedures to follow in visiting the destination?

Minutes searching: N/A

21. Can you find a photograph of a visitor at this website that looks like you?

Minutes searching: 4   Yes ()   No (x)   Not sure ()

Comments: No.

22. Can you information about what to do in case of a health or police emergency at this website?

Minutes searching: 4   Yes (x)   No ()   Not sure ()

Comments: Under Practical Information, "Health and Safety" – it recommends insurance, vaccinations, medical checklist – tells you what do to in case of crime, loss and/or scams. Much of this information is general/ precautionary – it details each malady in depth, including HIV, AIDS, and bird flu.

23. Does the website include specific information about shopping and specific stores to buy luxury goods?

Minutes searching: 5   Yes ()   No (x)   Not sure ()

Comments: If you buy a tourism guide, the information is listed there.

24. Does the website allow buying of specific products offered by specific stores via this official website?

Minutes searching: 5   Yes ( )   No (x)   Not sure ( )

Comments: It does suggest a guide for purchase.

25. Does the website tell about the night clubs and night life?

Minutes searching: 5   Yes ( )   No (x)   Not sure ( )

Comments: Again, if you purchase a tourism book, this information is included.

26. Does the website permit booking to specific night clubs and night life events?

Minutes searching: 4   Yes ( )   No (x)   Not sure ( )

Comments: No booking on this site.

27. Does this website provide information for handicapped, impaired, visitors/customers/students?

Minutes searching: 4   Yes ( )   No (x)   Not sure ( )

Comments: No.

28. Is there a calendar of openings, holidays, closings, and/or special events at this website?

Minutes searching: 10   Yes ( )   No (x)   Not sure ( )

Comments: It's a shame they don't list it here it could be very helpful. The only mention of holidays is at the bottom of "when to go" – it says hotels and tickets will be most expensive during Chinese New Year, May Day (a week long event beginning May 1) and National Holiday (first week in October). It says it will be "daunting to maneuver around 1.3 billion Chinese" during this time.

29. Is current weather available as well as weather by month of year at this website?

Minutes searching: 12   Yes, current weather ( )   Yes, for all months (x)
                    No current weather (x)   No weather for each   Not sure ( )
                                              month ( )

Comments: The site lists "when to go" in terms of weather.

30. Is the website available in languages other than English?

Minutes searching: 15 s   Yes (x)   No ()   Not sure ()

31. If yes, list all languages available at website:

English, Dutch, French, Spanish, Italian, Chinese, and Japanese

Comments: The icon is located at the bottom of the website "international."

32. Is historical information available at website?

Minutes searching: 1   YES (x)   No ()   Not sure ()

Comments: TONS of Chinese history. Pages and pages of valuable information.

33. Is one or more slideshows of still photographs shown at the website?

Minutes searching: 4   Yes (x)   No ()   Not sure ()

Comments: Pictures/slideshows can be found in the same area as the videos.

34. Is one or more videos shown at the website?

Minutes searching: 1   Yes (x)   No ()   Not sure ()   If yes, how many videos?

Comments: See above comments for specific video topics.

35. Is safety/security information given at the website?

Minutes searching: 2   Yes (x)   No ()   Not sure ()

Comments: See above comments, site lists detailed, and relevant information.

36. Does this website give visa requirements information?

Minutes searching: 6   Yes (x)   No ()   Not sure ()

Comments: Lots and lots of information:

Visas

For China

Apart from for citizens of Japan, Singapore, and Brunei, all visitors to China require a visa. A Chinese visa covers virtually the whole of China, although there are still some restricted areas that require an additional permit from the PSB. Permits are also required for travel to

Tibet, an area of China that the authorities can suddenly bar foreigners from entering.

At the time of writing, prices for a standard 30-day visa was US$50 for the US citizens and US$30 for the citizens of other nations. For double-entry visas, it's US$75 for the US citizens and US$45 for all other nationals. For multiple-entry visas for 6 months, it's US$100 for the US citizens and US$60 for all other nationals. A standard 30-day single-entry visa can be issued from most Chinese embassies abroad in 3–5 working days. Express visas cost twice the usual fee.

A 30-day visa is activated on the date you enter China, and must be used within 3 months of the date of issue. Sixty- and 90-day travel visas are less likely to be issued, although travelers have reported obtaining them with few problems. You need to extend your visa in China if you want to stay longer.

You normally pay for your visa when you collect it. You can get an application form in person at the embassy or consulate, or obtain one on-line from a consular website (try www.fmprc.gov.cn/eng – click on About China, then Travel to China, and then Visa Information). A visa mailed to you will take up to 3 weeks. Visa applications require at least one photo (normally 51 mm × 51 mm).

In some countries (e.g., the UK and the USA), the visa service has been outsourced from the Chinese embassy to a visa-issuing centre, which levies an extra administration fee. In the case of the UK, a single-entry visa costs £35, but the standard administration charge levied by the centre is a further £30. In the USA, many people use the China Visa Service Center (In the USA 800 799 6560; www.mychinavisa.com), which offers prompt service. The procedure takes around 10–14 days.

Hong Kong is still the best place to pick up a visa for China. China Travel Service (CTS) will be able to obtain one for you, or you can apply directly to the Visa Office of the People's Republic of China (3413 2300; 7th fl, Lower Block, China Resources Centre, 26 Harbour Rd, Wan Chai; 9 am-noon & 2–5 pm Mon-Fri). Visas processed here in 1/2/3 days cost HK$400/300/150. Double-entry visas are HK$220, while 6-month/1-year multiple-entry visas are HK$400/600 (plus HK$150/250 for express/urgent service). Be aware that American and UK passport holders must pay considerably more for their visas. You must supply two photos, which can be taken at photo booths in the Mass Transit Railway (MTR) or at the visa office for HK$35.

Five-day visas are available at the Luóhú border crossing between Hong Kong and Shēnzhèn. They are valid for Shēnzhèn only, however, and at the time of writing the US citizens still had to apply in advance in Hong Kong or already have a visa. Three-day visas are also available at the Macau–Zhūhǎi border (MOP$150 for most nationalities, MOP$450 for British) between 8.30 am and 10 pm. The US citizens have to buy a visa in advance in Macau or Hong Kong.

Be aware that political events can suddenly make visas more difficult to procure or renew. In the run-up to the Olympic Games in 2008, restrictions were imposed on certain types of visas; multiple-entry visas were not issued; some travelers were only given 7-day travel visas; extensions became difficult to procure; and other travelers were flatly denied visas. Embassies were also insisting that travelers provided details of their air tickets and accommodation in China.

Similarly, when asked about your itinerary on the application form, try to list standard tourist destinations such as Běijīng and Hángzhōu; if you are toying with the idea of going to Tibet or western Xīnjiāng, just leave it off the form. The list you give is not binding in any way.

When you check into a hotel, there is a question on the registration form asking what type of visa you hold. The letter specifying what type of visa you have is usually stamped on the visa itself. There are eight categories of visa (C – flight attendant, chéngwù, 乘务; D – resident, dìngjū, 定居; F – business or student, fǎngwèn, 访问; G – transit, guòjìng, 过境; J – journalist, jìzhě, 记者; L – travel, lǚxíng, 旅行; X – long-term student, liúxué, 留学; and Z – working, gōngzuò, 工作). For most travelers, the type of visa issued is an L.

For Hong Kong

At the time of writing, most visitors to Hong Kong, including citizens of the EU, Australia, New Zealand, the USA, and Canada, could enter and stay for 90 days without a visa. British passport holders get 180 days, while South Africans are allowed to stay 30 days without a visa. If you do require a visa, apply at a Chinese embassy or consulate before arriving. Be aware that if you visit Hong Kong from China, you will need to either have a multiple-entry visa to re-enter China or get a new visa.

For Macau

Most travelers, including citizens of the EU, Australia, New Zealand, the USA, Canada, and South Africa, can enter Macau without a visa for between 30 and 90 days. Most other nationalities can get a 30-day visa on arrival, which will cost MOP$100/50/200 per adult/child under 12/family. If you're visiting Macau from China and plan to re-enter China, you will need to be on a multiple-entry visa.

Visa Extensions
The Foreign Affairs Branch of the local PSB; Gōngānjú – the police force – deals with visa extensions.

First-time extensions of 30 days are easy to obtain on single-entry tourist visas, but further extensions are harder to get and may only give you another week. Offices of the PSB outside of Běijīng may be more lenient and more willing to offer further extensions, but don't bank on it.

Extensions to single-entry visas vary in price, depending on your nationality. American travelers pay Y185, Canadians Y165, UK citizens Y160, and Australians Y100; prices can go up or down. Expect to wait up to 5 days for your visa extension to be processed.

The period of extension can differ from city to town. Travelers report generous extensions being decided on the spot in provincial towns and backwaters. If you have used up all your options, popping into Hong Kong to apply for a new tourist visa is a reliable option.

The penalty for overstaying your visa in China is up to Y500 per day. Some travelers have reported having trouble with officials who read the "valid until" date on their visa incorrectly. For a one-month tourist (L) visa, the "valid until" date is the date by which you must enter the country (within three months of the date the visa was issued), not the date upon which your visa expires. Your visa expires the number of days that your visa is valid for after the date of entry into China.

Residence Permit
The "green card" is a residence permit, issued to English teachers, foreign expats, and long-term students who live in China. Green cards are issued for a period of 6 months to 1 year and must be renewed annually. Besides needing all the right paperwork, you (and your spouse) must also pass a health exam (for which there is a charge). Families are automatically included once the permit is issued, but there is a fee for each family member. If you lose your card, you'll pay a hefty fee to have it replaced.

Poland Government Rubric

Researcher's Name: Christopher P. Dion
Date: 4/05/2010

Website brand: Government-sponsored
Website address: http://www.poland.travel/en/

This site was more in line with the previous government-sponsored sites. I consider Russia to be a glitch, or perhaps indicative of Russia's approach to tourism itself (get your reservations down/visas applied for). The pictures for Poland looked beautiful!! We are going to Poland as I mentioned in my presentation. This site also featured a newbie for rubric success: Ordering mailings about the country, which would not have arrived in a reasonable time period. You can request information about Poland and Poland Cultural and Heritage, free posters, maps, Poland for the young visitors, Poland camping, Poland for Health and Beauty, Polish Cuisine, Polish Cities and National Parks, among others. This site also had the most extensive language options (see 31). I love how it said Polish hospitality is unparalleled in the world – "every host wants to be the host with the most" – see customs and manners comments at end of rubric as additional section. Overall, this site dwarfed the lonely planet site as well.

Issues:

Can I book a moderately priced hotel room at this website for a 10-day visit in mid-June 2010? ($150 per night)

Minutes searching for answer: 3   Yes (x)   No ()   Not sure ()

Comments: Tons of hotels available under 150/night.

What do I get for this hotel room (free internet?; use of exercise room?; swimming pool?)

Minutes searching: 3   Not sure ()   1–3 amenities ()   4+ amenities (x)

Comments: Spa, sauna, hot tub, AC, gift shop, Internet, bar and tearoom, satellite TV.

3. Does the official site tell me what special events are available in mid-June 2010?

Minutes searching for answer: 3   Yes (x)   No ()   Not sure ()

Comments: There is a calendar of events, shown by month with events listed daily. Great info and a huge perk for the site.

4. If yes, can I book one of these events on-line at the official website?

Minutes searching: 6   Yes ( )   No (x)   Not sure ( )

Comments: (Describe events) Too many to list. Click on link below:

http://www.poland.travel/en/events-calendar/monthly-view/06-06-2010/

5. Can I become a "member" at this website? (If yes, do become a member if membership if free.)

Minutes searching: 2   Yes ( )   No (x)   Not sure ( )

Comments: Everything you see is free, including mailings.

6. Can I pay to become a special member (e.g., pay dues) at this website?

Minutes searching: Yes ( )   No (x)   Not sure ( )

Comments: This is a free site.

7. What do I get for membership at the website?

Minutes searching: 2   N/A

Comments:

8. Does the website tell me what unique "must do" attractions that I should visit in June?

Minutes searching: 5   Yes (x)   No ( )   Not sure ( )

Comments: See #3.

9. Can I book one of these attractions at the official website?

Minutes searching: 2   Yes ( )   No (x)   Not sure ( )

Comments: The website links to many other websites.

10. Does the website offer free paper copy literature that will be mailed to me?

Minutes searching: 4   Yes (x)   No ( )   Not sure ( )

Comments: They offer tons of free information. Poland seems very friendly and open already.

If yes, request this literature and record the date of the request and when you receive the literature. N/A.

11. Are videos shown at this website?

Minutes searching: 3   Yes (x)   No ()   Not sure ()

Comments: Yes! 11 pages of videos.

12. If yes, can I select a video that shows visitors doing things that I prefer to do at this destination?

Minutes searching: 2   Yes (x)   No ()   Not sure ()

Comments: Horse riding in Mazowsze, tons of "visit Poland" videos, many highlights of attractions.

13. Can I see a map of the destination at the website?

Minutes searching: 2   Yes (x)   No ()   Not sure ()

Comments:

Can I request a map be sent to me via mail from this website?

Minutes searching: 2   Yes (x)   No ()   Not sure ()

Comments: Tons of literature mailed for free, see initial comments.

16. Can I book a classical upscale restaurant at the official website?

Minutes searching: 5   Yes ()   No (x)   Not sure ()

Comments:

Minutes to book: N/A   Easy to do ()   Hard to do ()   Not sure ()

Comments: N/A.

18. Does the website offer information for visits by families with young children?

Minutes searching: 5   Yes (x)   No ()   Not sure ()

Comments: And it offers free literature mailings for things to do with families as well.

19. Can the visitor to the website ask for a mailing of literature about visiting for a family of two adults and two children 4 and 9 years old?

Minutes searching: 5   Yes (x)   No ()   Not sure ()

Comments:

20. Does the website offer an interactive game to play?

Minutes searching: 2   Yes ( )   No (x)   Not sure ( )

Comments:

If yes, does the game provide further information about the destination and trip procedures to follow in visiting the destination?

Minutes searching: N/A

21. Can you find a photograph of a visitor at this website that looks like you?

Minutes searching: 6   Yes ( )   No (x)   Not sure ( )

Comments:

22. Can you information about what to do in case of a health or police emergency at this website?

Minutes searching: 2   Yes (x)   No ( )   Not sure ( )

Comments:

A trip to Poland is above all a chance to rest, relax, and have fun. However, anywhere you go you may encounter situations which turn out to be less pleasant. Therefore before setting off it is worth finding out some basic information about how to cope with unforeseen events.

Emergency numbers

Here are the important emergency contact numbers in Poland:

To call an emergency service using a landline or a public phone, please dial

999 – Ambulance
998 – Fire Brigade
997 – Police
986 – Municipal Wardens (Straż Miejska)
To call an emergency service using a mobile phone, please dial
112 – All services

As soon as the call is connected, you will be transferred to the appropriate service. You may also use this number if you are unsure which of the three emergency numbers (997, 998, 999) should be alerted.

Calling water and mountain rescue services (WOPR, GOPR)

In Poland, you can also contact special rescue services responsible for lifesaving operations in the mountains and on lakes and waterways:

Mountain rescue service (GOPR) – +48 601 100 300
Water rescue service (WOPR) – +48 601 100 100

Please note: the numbers above should be used only in cases of emergency – never to obtain tourist information.

23. Does the website include specific information about shopping and specific stores to buy luxury goods?

Minutes searching: Yes (x)   No ()   Not sure ()
Comments:

24. Does the website allow buying of specific products offered by specific stores via this official website?

Minutes searching: 5   Yes ()   No (x)   Not sure ()
Comments:

25. Does the website tell about the night clubs and night life?

Minutes searching: 3   Yes ()   No (x)   Not sure ()
Comments:

26. Does the website permit booking to specific night clubs and night life events?

Minutes searching: 4   Yes ()   No (x)   Not sure ()
Comments:

27. Does this website provide information for handicapped, impaired, visitors/customers/students?

Minutes searching: 3   Yes ()   No (x)   Not sure ()
Comments:

28. Is there a calendar of openings, holidays, closings, and/or special events at this website?

Minutes searching: 3   Yes (x)   No ()   Not sure ()
Comments: Yes, a very detailed calendar of events, see above comments.

29. Is current weather available as well as weather by month of year at this website?

Minutes searching: 12 Yes, current weather (x) Yes, for all months ()
                                 No current weather ()   No weather for each   Not sure ()
                                                    month (x)

Comments: Current weather conditions listed on the main page.

30. Is the website available in languages other than English?

Minutes searching: 15 s   Yes (x)   No ()   Not sure ()

31. If yes, list all languages available at website:

English, Chinese, Japanese, French, Dutch, German, Polish, Swedish, Hungarian, Osterreich German dialect, and Greek

Comments: Top R hand corner.

32. Is historical information available at website?

Minutes searching: 1   Yes (x)   No ()   Not sure ()

Comments: Tons of historical information. (11 pages).

33. Is one or more slideshows of still photographs shown at the website?

Minutes searching: 4   Yes (x)   No ()   Not sure ()

Comments: Pictures/slideshows on this website are beautiful.

34. Is one or more videos shown at the website?

Minutes searching: 1   Yes (x)   No ()   Not sure ()   If yes, how many videos?

Comments: Pages and pages of video highlights.

35. Is safety/security information given at the website?

Minutes searching: 2   Yes (x)   No ()   Not sure ()

Comments: See above comments (#22), site lists detailed information.

36. Does this website give visa requirements information?

Minutes searching: 10   Yes (x)   No ()   Not sure ()
Comments: Great info:

Visas-general information

There are many countries whose citizens can visit Poland as tourists without visas. These include all European Union countries.

Visa free travel to Poland is available to citizens of many countries outside the European Union.

Countries whose citizens can travel to Poland for up to 90 days without a visa:

Andorra, Argentina, Australia, Austria, Belgium, Bolivia, Brazil, Brunei, Bulgaria, Canada, Chile, Costa Rica, Croatia, Cyprus, Czech Republic, Denmark, El Salvador, Estonia, Finland, France, Germany, Greece, Guatemala, Honduras, Hong Kong (SAR), Hungary, Iceland, Ireland, Israel, Italy, Japan, Latvia, Liechtenstein, Lithuania, Luxembourg, Macao (SAR), Malaysia, Malta, Mexico, Monaco, Netherlands, New Zealand, Nicaragua, Norway, Panama, Paraguay, Portugal, Romania, San Marino, Singapore, Slovakia, Slovenia, South Korea, Spain, Sweden, Switzerland, United Kingdom, the United States of America, Uruguay, Vatican, and Venezuela.

Detailed information on rules covering entry and stay in Poland can be obtained from Polish embassies and consular offices.

A list of addresses of embassies and consulates.

A visa is still required for a stay of longer than 3 months or when entering the country to take up paid employment.

A list of countries whose citizens can travel to Poland for up to 90 days without a visa.

Additional information worth noting: Customs and manners:

From the ancient custom of greeting visitors with bread and salt, Poland's system of social graces has developed into one that is unmatched in the world, and will often put a smile on your face. You can expect to be spoilt – every Pole wants to be the host with the most, no money and effort spared.

When in Poland, be prepared for your words to be sometimes misinterpreted, but do not worry about communication. You will find it very easy to engage in a friendly conversation, even regardless of the other speaker's linguistic competence.

You will be overwhelmed by the exceptional hospitality offered by the Polish people and the good-hearted everyday social rituals you will experience.

When visiting a traditional Polish home, be prepared to be confronted with situations described below:

- Even on the first visit do not be surprised to be offered by your host a pair of slippers for your comfort.
- If you are invited for dinner, better go on an empty stomach because otherwise you will find it difficult to feast on a generous helping of soup with noodles, pork cutlet with cabbage and potatoes, topped with a cheesecake and washed with a bottle of home distilled flavored liquor.
- If you abstain from alcohol, you will find that in Poland it is sometimes not enough just to say "no, thanks," as your host may assume his traditional Polish hospitality is being put to test.
- If you travel on public transport, be prepared for a display of old fashioned courtesy: young people give up their places to the elderly, while gentlemen make way for ladies.
- It is considered exceptionally courteous to kiss a woman's hand as a way of greeting. This practice is particularly popular among the older generation.
- While dining in a restaurant, you will be expected to leave a tip. Tipping is similar to the rest of Europe, i.e. at least 10% of the value of the bill.

There are, of course, many more specifically Polish customs. It is also worth knowing that the Poles are a particularly friendly and supportive people, who cultivate a sense of duty toward each other and their families and friends.

Since 95% of the population are Roman Catholics, all major church holidays are strictly observed, particularly Christmas and Easter. On such occasion, Polish families come together to enjoy good food and drink.

Poland Private Sector Rubric

Researcher's Name: Christopher P. Dion
Date: 4/05/2010

Website brand: Lonely Planet (Global)
Website address: http://www.lonelyplanet.com/poland

Issues:

Can I book a moderately priced hotel room at this website for a 10-day visit in mid-June 2010? ($150 per night)

Minutes searching for answer: 3   Yes (x)   No ()   Not sure ()

Comments: Almost every hotel was under the $150 price range in my first search, including 5 star hotels for around $100. The hotels in Poland listed appear really nice.

What do I get for this hotel room (free internet?; use of exercise room?; swimming pool?)

Minutes searching: 3   Not sure ()   1–3 amenities ()   4+ amenities (x)

Comments: Spa, sauna, hot tub, AC, gift shop, Internet, bar and tearoom, satellite TV.

3. Does the official site tell me what special events are available in mid-June 2010?

Minutes searching for answer: 5   Yes (x)   No ()   Not sure ()

Comments: Opole's National Festival of Polish Song exists exclusively in June since 1963, Sea Days festival is in June, encompassing fireworks, concerts, songs, and performances.

4. If yes, can I book one of these events on-line at the official website?

Minutes searching: 6   Yes ()   No (x)   Not sure ()

Comments: (Describe events) There were links to other sites to book events, but lonely planet did describe in detail the Aquarium, dance halls, among others.

5. Can I become a "member" at this website? (If yes, do become a member if membership if free.)

Minutes searching: 2   Yes (x)   No ()   Not sure ()

Comments: It's free to be a member.

6. Can I pay to become a special member (e.g., pay dues) at this website?

Minutes searching: Yes ()   No (x)   Not sure ()

Comments: This is a free site.

7. What do I get for membership at the website?

Minutes searching: 2   Multiple perks (x)   No ()   Not sure ()

Comments: Get and share tips, find groups to travel with, save trip places and itineraries, rate and review places you've been.

8. Does the website tell me what unique "must do" attractions that I should visit in June?

Minutes searching: 5   Yes (x)   No ()   Not sure ()

Comments: See #3.

9. Can I book one of these attractions at the official website?

Minutes searching: 2   Yes ()   No (x)   Not sure ()

Comments: The website links to many other websites.

10. Does the website offer free paper copy literature that will be mailed to me?

Minutes searching: 4   Yes ()   No (x)   Not sure ()

Comments: Travel guides can be purchased. You can sign up for an on-line newsletter as well.

If yes, request this literature and record the date of the request and when you receive the literature. N/A.

11. Are videos shown at this website?

Minutes searching: 3   Yes (x)   No ()   Not sure ()

Comments: There are travel videos about Warsaw and Krakow and several slideshows.

12. If yes, can I select a video that shows visitors doing things that I prefer to do at this destination?

Minutes searching: 2   Yes (x)   No ()   Not sure ()

Comments: The videos give you an "insider view" on Warsaw and Krakow's best sites, districts and surprises.

13. Can I see a map of the destination at the website?

Minutes searching: 2   Yes (x)   No ()   Not sure ()

Comments: Click on "show map" – This map is similar to the other lonely planet maps and displays satellite, hybrid, and terrain, with all major cities marked with blue flags.

Can I request a map be sent to me via mail from this website?

Minutes searching: 2   Yes ()   No (x)   Not sure ()

Comments: Not possible on this site.

16. Can I book a classical upscale restaurant at the official website?

Minutes searching: 5   Yes ()   No (x)   Not sure ()

Comments: It does suggest areas to visit for upscale restaurants, but you cannot book a table on this site.

Minutes to book: N/A   Easy to do ()   Hard to do ()   Not sure ()

Comments: N/A.

18. Does the website offer information for visits by families with young children?

Minutes searching: 5   Yes ()   No (x)   Not sure ()

Comments: The only "family" discussions are those of aristocratic Polish summer palaces.

19. Can the visitor to the website ask for a mailing of literature about visiting for a family of two adults and two children 4 and 9 years old?

Minutes searching: 5   Yes ()   No (x)   Not sure ()

Comments: This website does not mail literature for free.

20. Does the website offer an interactive game to play?

Minutes searching: 2   Yes ()   No (x)   Not sure ()

Comments:

If yes, does the game provide further information about the destination and trip procedures to follow in visiting the destination?

Minutes searching: N/A

21. Can you find a photograph of a visitor at this website that looks like you?

Minutes searching: 6   Yes ()   No (x)   Not sure ()

Comments: The videos and slideshows feature the Poles.

22. Can you information about what to do in case of a health or police emergency at this website?

Minutes searching: 2   Yes (x)   No ()   Not sure ()

Comments: Under health and safety, it discusses insurance, vaccinations, dangers, and annoyances. It lists Poland as a relatively safe country to visit but distinguishes Warsaw as the least safe city. It also describes heavy drinking and smoking as a way of life in Poland, and although the service is slow and impolite in general, this is starting to change. It is interesting that it points out that young boys holding out bags are not begging but rather are collecting for the boy scouts. It also explains that Poland is a homogenous nation and that looks, stares and "giggles" from its inhabitants can be expected. Another interesting precaution: Poles do not like to stop at zebra crossings, be careful when you step out on the road. I would claim this section to be among the lonely planet's strengths.

23. Does the website include specific information about shopping and specific stores to buy luxury goods?

Minutes searching: Yes ()   No (x)   Not sure ()

Comments: If you buy a lonely planet tourism guide, the information is listed there.

24. Does the website allow buying of specific products offered by specific stores via this official website?

Minutes searching: 5   Yes ()   No (x)   Not sure ()

Comments: It does suggest a shopping guide for purchase.

25. Does the website tell about the night clubs and night life?

Minutes searching: 3   Yes (x)   No ()   Not sure ()

Comments: Indirectly, it is listed through user reviews and comments. Detailed information though, which would be helpful to an international traveler.

26. Does the website permit booking to specific night clubs and night life events?

Minutes searching: 4   Yes ()   No (x)   Not sure ()
Comments: Again they want you to purchase their books.

27. Does this website provide information for handicapped, impaired, visitors/customers/students?

Minutes searching: 3   Yes (x)   No ()   Not sure ()

Comments: Very limited information, indirectly provided through user reviews, 1 result came up discussing the Wieliczka salt mine's elevator (it also included Wieliczka's website with more information for handicapped visitors).

28. Is there a calendar of openings, holidays, closings, and/or special events at this website?

Minutes searching: 3   Yes ()   No (x)   Not sure ()

Comments: There is not a specific calendar but many holidays are discussed in user reviews.

29. Is current weather available as well as weather by month of year at this website?

Minutes searching: 12   Yes, current weather ()   Yes, for all months (x)
                        No current weather (x)   No weather for each   Not sure ()
                                                 month ()

Comments: Weather is discussed extensively under "when to go." User reviews also chime in with a few tips.

30. Is the website available in languages other than English?

Minutes searching: 15 s   Yes (x)   No ()   Not sure ()

31. If yes, list all languages available at website:

English, Dutch, French, Spanish, Italian, Chinese, and Japanese

Comments: The icon is located at the bottom of the website "international."

32. Is historical information available at website?

Minutes searching: 1   Yes (x)   No ()   Not sure ()

Comments: Historical information is detailed and poetic at times: "Forever sandwiched between two powerful aggressors, it has. ..." Lonely planet has better than your run of the mill historical information writers. Historical information commences with "before the Poles."

33. Is one or more slideshows of still photographs shown at the website?

Minutes searching: 4   Yes (x)   No ()   Not sure ()

Comments: Pictures/slideshows were listed in this website.

34. Is one or more videos shown at the website?

Minutes searching: 1   Yes (x)   No ()   Not sure ()   If yes, how many videos?

Comments: Videos highlights of Warsaw and Krakow.

35. Is safety/security information given at the website?

Minutes searching: 2   Yes (x)   No ()   Not sure ()

Comments: See above comments (#22), site lists detailed information.

36. Does this website give visa requirements information?

Minutes searching: 10   Yes ()   No (x)   Not sure ()

Comments: You do not need a visa to travel in Poland. A valid passport is all that is required, so says lonely planet.

Thailand Government Sponsored Rubric

Researcher's Name: Christopher P. Dion
Research Assistant: Sheri Dion
Date: 4/05/2010

Website brand: Government-sponsored
Website address: TourismThailand.org

This site dwarfs the lonely planet's information as well. There are ample videos, 7 interactive games, slideshows, historical, and relevant information. This was the only site I've researched that has had interactive games and a day-by-day calendar of holidays/closings.

Issues:

Can I book a moderately priced hotel room at this website for a 10 day visit in mid-June 2010? ($150 per night)

Minutes searching for answer: 6   Yes (x)   No ()   Not sure ()

Comments: Multiple destinations.

What do I get for this hotel room (free internet?; use of exercise room?; swimming pool?)

Minutes searching: 4   Not sure ()   1–3 amenities ()   4+ amenities (x)

Comments: More than 4 for each hotel.

3. Does the official site tell me what special events are available in mid-June 2010?

Minutes searching for answer: 6   Yes (x)   No ()   Not sure ()

Comments: Yes, it has a calendar for each month's events, festivals, and activities. Examples: June.

Festivals & Events
    Home > Festivals & Events

3 Jun–6 Sep 2010
French Thai Cultural Festival in Bangkok

Phi Ta Khon Festival
Phi Ta Khon Festival
12 Jun–14 Jun 2010
The Phi Ta Khon festival is unique to the Dan Sai district in Loei Province and reflects the local I ...

Thailand Tourism Festival
1 Jun–30 Jun 2010
At 40,000 square meters, the Thailand Tourism Festival (TTF) is billed as the country's largest festival.

4. If yes, can I book one of these events on-line at the official website?

Minutes searching: 8   Yes ()   No (x)   Not sure ()

Comments: (Describe events) See (#3) above.

5. Can I become a "member" at this website? (If yes, do become a member if membership if free.)

Minutes searching: 2   Yes (x)   No ()   Not sure ()

Comments: It differentiates between Tourism, Business and Media/Press Member. Business and Media/Press signups require TAT approval.

6. Can I pay to become a special member (e.g., pay dues) at this website?

Minutes searching: Yes ()   No (x)   Not sure ()

Comments: This is a free site.

7. What do I get for membership at the website?

Minutes searching: 2   Multiple perks (x)   No ()   Not sure ()

Comments: Tourism member: Free e-newsletter and Thailand itinerary planner. Business member: Signing up to Thailand Travel Directory the center of all Thailand tourism business relate and tourism product. For Media/Press: Signing up to get extract tourism news for press.

8. Does the website tell me what unique "must do" attractions that I should visit in June?

Minutes searching: 10   Yes (x)   No ()   Not sure ()

Comments: This site is great. See above.

9. Can I book one of these attractions at the official website?

Minutes searching: 2   Yes ()   No (x)   Not sure ()

Comments: Yes and no. The site provides phone numbers for more information, but most are free and do not need to be booked.

10. Does the website offer free paper copy literature that will be mailed to me?

Minutes searching: 4   Yes ()   No (x)   Not sure ()

Comments: Sign up for e-newsletters.

If yes, request this literature and record the date of the request and when you receive the literature. N/A.

11. Are videos shown at this website?

Minutes searching: 3   Yes (x)   No ()   Not sure ()

Comments: Yes, TONS of videos. These dwarf the quantity on the lonely planet – 9 pages of videos!! (12 per page).

12. If yes, can I select a video that shows visitors doing things that I prefer to do at this destination?

Minutes searching: 4   Yes (x)   No ()   Not sure ()

Comments: Yes, the videos are numbered, so pick the number you'd like to see.

13. Can I see a map of the destination at the website?

Minutes searching: 2   Yes (x)   No ()   Not sure ()

Comments: Detailed with cities.

Can I request a map be sent to me via mail from this website?

Minutes searching: 4   Yes ()   No (x)   Not sure ()

Comments: E-newsletters/magazines only.

16. Can I book a classical upscale restaurant at the official website?

Minutes searching: 5   Yes ()   No (x)   Not sure ()

Comments: No.

Minutes to book: N/A   Easy to do ()   Hard to do ()   Not sure ()

Comments: N/A.

18. Does the website offer information for visits by families with young children?

Minutes searching: 8   Yes (x)   No ()   Not sure ()

Comments: Activities are generalized as things to see, not necessarily great for families – but many activities would indeed facilitate families. My answer would have to be yes and no.

From this profusion of location and activity, the Tourism Authority of Thailand (TAT) is identifying new attractions and promoting niche markets, special programs with appeal to special interests and needs: to younger travelers, to families, to honeymoon couples, to cultural travelers, to voyagers seeking health and wellbeing holidays.

19. Can the visitor to the website ask for a mailing of literature about visiting for a family of two adults and two children 4 and 9 years old?

Minutes searching: 5   Yes (x)   No ()   Not sure ()

Comments: You can sign up for the e-newsletter, assuming articles in the newsletter would arise for this reason.

20. Does the website offer an interactive game to play?

Minutes searching: 2   Yes (x)   No ()   Not sure ()

Comments: There are seven games: Shopping, Photo, Massage, LolKa Tong, Diving, River Racing, and Somtum.

If yes, does the game provide further information about the destination and trip procedures to follow in visiting the destination?

Minutes searching: Yes. A cute idea. My favorite was the river racing.

21. Can you find a photograph of a visitor at this website that looks like you?

Minutes searching: 6   Yes (x)   No ( )   Not sure ( )

Comments: "Looks like me" again equivocates to "American."

22. Can you information about what to do in case of a health or police emergency at this website?

Minutes searching: 4   Yes (x)   No ( )   Not sure ( )

Comments: Medical Services.

All tourism destinations and provincial capitals have hospitals and clinics staffed by well-trained doctors and nurse. In the case of an emergency, an ambulance can be summoned from any private hospital.

Vaccinations: As in most other countries, visitors do not require vaccinations unless coming from or passing through a designated contaminated area.

23. Does the website include specific information about shopping and specific stores to buy luxury goods?

Minutes searching: Yes ( )   No (x)   Not sure ( )

Comments: Only generalized shopping information is available.

Giant markets like Chatuchak and Suan Lum Night Bazaar also sell international brand names, but their fame rests on their diversity. From local fashions and handicrafts at giveaway prices, the range of discoveries to be made there is quite astounding.

Everywhere in Thailand traditional products are hand made by local artisans: weavers of cotton and silk, wood carvers, potters working in the local clay, silversmiths, basket makers, and cooks making local gourmet specialties.

24. Does the website allow buying of specific products offered by specific stores via this official website?

Minutes searching: 5   Yes ( )   No (x)   Not sure ( )

Comments: No.

25. Does the website tell about the night clubs and night life?

Minutes searching: 5   Yes ( )   No (x)   Not sure ( )

Comments: Not too much info about specific night clubs.

26. Does the website permit booking to specific night clubs and night life events?

Minutes searching: 4   Yes ( )   No (x)   Not sure ( )

Comments: N/A.

27. Does this website provide information for handicapped, impaired, visitors/customers/students?

Minutes searching: 5   Yes ( )   No (x)   Not sure ( )

Comments: A lack of information on both sites.

28. Is there a calendar of openings, holidays, closings, and/or special events at this website?

Minutes searching: 4   Yes (x)   No ( )   Not sure ( )

Comments: There is a day-by-day monthly calendar which lists this information. See "Calendar."

29. Is current weather available as well as weather by month of year at this website?

Minutes searching: 12 Yes, current weather (x) Yes, for all months ( )
                       No current weather (x)   No weather for each   Not sure ( )
                                                month ( )

Comments: The site lists current weather and forecasts for all areas.

30. Is the website available in languages other than English?

Minutes searching: 15 s   Yes (x)   No ( )   Not sure ( )

31. If yes, list all languages available at website:

English, Thai – it also has an "other language" designation – but the "other language" options, I could not procure.

Comments: Located at top of site.

32. Is historical information available at website?

Minutes searching: 1   Yes (x)   No ()   Not sure ()

Comments: Under "historical."

33. Is one or more slideshows of still photographs shown at the website?

Minutes searching: 4   Yes (x)   No ()   Not sure ()

Comments: Many pictures/slideshows were listed in this website.

34. Is one or more videos shown at the website?

Minutes searching: 1   Yes (x)   No ()   Not sure ()   If yes, how many videos?

Comments: There are early a hundred videos on this site.

35. Is safety/security information given at the website?

Minutes searching: 2   Yes (x)   No ()   Not sure ()

Comments: Below are additional comments to those listed above.

Special Advice:

- Beware of unauthorized people who offer their services as guides. For all tourist information, contact the Tourism Authority of Thailand, Tel: 1672. For information about Bangkok, contact the Bangkok Metropolitan Tourist Bureau, Tel: 0 2225 7612-4.
- Observe all normal precautions as regards to personal safety, as well as the safety of your belongings. Walking alone on quiet streets or deserted areas is not recommended. Be sure that all your valuables – money, jewelry, and airline tickets are properly protected from loss. Visitors needing assistance relating to safety, unethical practices, or other matters, please call the Tourist Police at Tel: 1155.
- Drop your garbage into a waste container. The Bangkok Metropolitan Administration id no strictly enforcing the law in an effort to keep the city

clean and healthy. The fine will be imposed on a person who spits, discards cigarette stubs, or drops rubbish in public areas.
– Do not get yourself involved with drugs. Penalties for drug offences are very severe in Thailand.
– Do not support any manner of wild animal abuse. Never purchase any products or souvenirs made from wild animals including reptiles like snakes, monitor lizards, and also turtle shell and ivory. Avoid patronizing local restaurants that serve wild animal delicacies. It is against the law to slaughter wildlife for food in Thailand.

36. Does this website give visa requirements information?

Minutes searching: 1   Yes (x)   No ()   Not sure ()

Comments: General information.

As a general rule, any foreigner seeking entry into the Kingdom of Thailand for business, investment, study, medical treatment, mass media, religion, employment, and other purposes is required to apply for a visa from a Thai Embassy or Consulate-General. To do so, a foreigner must possess a valid passport or travel document that is recognized by the Royal Thai Government and comply with the conditions set forth in the Immigration Act B.E.2522 (1979) and its related provisions.

Foreigners who fall into any of the following categories are prohibited to enter the Kingdom.

• Having no genuine and valid passport or document used in lieu of passport; or having a genuine and valid passport or document used in lieu of passport without visaing by the Royal Thai Embassies or Consulates in foreign countries; or from the Ministry of Foreign Affairs, except if a visa is not required for certain types of aliens in special instances. Visaing and visa exemption will be under the terms and conditions as provided in the Ministerial Regulations.
• Having no appropriate means of living following entrance into the Kingdom.
• Having entered into the Kingdom to take occupation as a laborer, or to take employment by using physical energy without skills or training, or to work in violation of the Alien Work Permit Law.
• Being mentally unstable or having any of the diseases as prescribed in the Ministerial Regulations.
• Having not yet been vaccinated against smallpox or inoculated or undergone any other medical treatment for protection against disease and

having refused to have such vaccinations administered by the Immigration Doctor.
- Having been imprisoned by the judgment of the Thai Court; or by a lawful injunction; or by the judgment of the Court of foreign country, except when the penalty is for petty offense or negligence or is provided for as an exception in the Ministerial Regulations.
- Having behavior which would indicate possible danger to the Public or likelihood of being nuisance or constituting any violence to the peace or safety of the public or to the security of the public or to the security of the nation, or being under warrant of arrest by competent officials of foreign governments.
- Reason to believe that entrance into the Kingdom was for the purpose of being involved in prostitution, the trading of women of children, drug smuggling, or other types of smuggling which are contrary to the public morality.
- Having no money or bond as prescribed by the Minister under Section 14 of the Immigration Act B.E. 2522.
- Being a person prohibited by the Minister under Section 16 of the Immigration Act B.E. 2522.
- Being deported by either the Government of Thailand that of or other foreign countries; or the right to stay in the Kingdom or in foreign countries having been revoked; or having been sent out of the Kingdom by competent officials at the expense of the Government of Thailand unless the Minister shall consider exemption on an individual special case basis.

The examination and diagnosis of disease of a physical or mental nature, including protective operations as against disease, shall be conducted by the Immigration Doctor.

Information on location and contact number of the Thai Embassy and Consulate-General abroad could be obtained from the Ministry of Foreign Affairs, Department of Consular Affairs, Visas, and Travel Documents Division, 123 Chaengwattana Road, Bangkok 10210, Tel. (662) 981-7171 ext. 3201-2, 3204-5 or direct line 575-1062-4, Fax. (662) 575-1066, E-mail: div1303@mfa.go.th

Note: Please check the period of stay stamped in your passport by the immigration officer. Visitors who overstay their visa will, at the time of their departure, be fined 500 baht for each excess day.

Thailand Private Sector Rubric

Researcher's Name: Christopher P. Dion
Date: 4/05/2010

Website brand: Lonely Planet (Global)
Website address: http://www.lonelyplanet.com/thailand

Issues:

Can I book a moderately priced hotel room at this website for a 10-day visit in mid-June 2010? ($150 per night)

Minutes searching for answer: 6   Yes (x)   No ()   Not sure ()

Comments: There are many, many destinations in Thailand under the $150 price range.

What do I get for this hotel room (free internet?; use of exercise room?; swimming pool?)

Minutes searching: 4   Not sure ()   1–3 amenities ()   4+amenities (x)

Comments: Swimming pool, sauna, fitness center, internet, and nightclub.

3. Does the official site tell me what special events are available in mid-June 2010?

Minutes searching for answer: 6   Yes (x)   No ()   Not sure ()

Comments: It mentions top things to do, see and visit in Thailand. It does have a link to tourism guidebooks, which include more information, but must be purchased.

4. If yes, can I book one of these events on-line at the official website?

Minutes searching: 8   Yes ()   No (x)   Not sure ()

Comments: (Describe events) Cooking classes in Chiang Mai, elephant jungle trek, and river rafting, to name a few can all be booked through a links to external websites.

5. Can I become a "member" at this website? (If yes, do become a member if membership if free.)

Minutes searching: 2   Yes (x)   No ()   Not sure ()

Comments: It's free to be a member.

6. Can I pay to become a special member (e.g., pay dues) at this website?

Minutes searching: Yes ( )   No (x)   Not sure ( )

Comments: It seems as though this is a free site.

7. What do I get for membership at the website?

Minutes searching: 2   Multiple perks (x)   No ( )   Not sure ( )

Comments: Get and share tips, find groups to travel with, save trip places and itineraries, rate and review places you've been.

8. Does the website tell me what unique "must do" attractions that I should visit in June?

Minutes searching: 10   Yes (x)   No ( )   Not sure ( )

Comments: From June to November, a waterfall flows and can be seen in Pha Taem National Park, orchids bloom in June in Khao Yai National Park, there is only water in the stream of a waterfall in Prsat Khao Phra Wihan National Park from June through October, "Python Rapids" rise only until the end of June, and Dan Sai's Phi Ta Khon Festival occurs only in June.

9. Can I book one of these attractions at the official website?

Minutes searching: 2   Yes ( )   No (x)   Not sure ( )

Comments: The website links to many other websites.

10. Does the website offer free paper copy literature that will be mailed to me?

Minutes searching: 4   Yes ( )   No (x)   Not sure ( )

Comments: Travel guides can be purchased. You can sign up for an on-line newsletter as well.

If yes, request this literature and record the date of the request and when you receive the literature. N/A.

11. Are videos shown at this website?

Minutes searching: 3   Yes (x)   No ( )   Not sure ( )

Comments: There are multiple travel videos.

12. If yes, can I select a video that shows visitors doing things that I prefer to do at this destination?

Minutes searching: 4   Yes (x)   No ()   Not sure ()

Comments: Detail of prayer bells, monks at Phra Pathom Chedi, riverboats, street stall vendors, Tuk-Tuks.

13. Can I see a map of the destination at the website?

Minutes searching: 2   Yes (x)   No ()   Not sure ()

Comments: Click on "show map."

Can I request a map be sent to me via mail from this website?

Minutes searching: 4   Yes ()   No (x)   Not sure ()

Comments: The map could feature more detail.

16. Can I book a classical upscale restaurant at the official website?

Minutes searching: 5   Yes ()   No (x)   Not sure ()

Comments: It does discuss that many restaurants are set up on certain islands, but you cannot reserve a table on this site.

Minutes to book: N/A   Easy to do ()   Hard to do ()   Not sure ()

Comments: N/A.

18. Does the website offer information for visits by families with young children?

Minutes searching: 8   Yes (x)   No ()   Not sure ()

Comments: It suggests Southeastern Thailand and the Lower Southern Gulf as being good family-friendly spots.

19. Can the visitor to the website ask for a mailing of literature about visiting for a family of two adults and two children 4 and 9 years old?

Minutes searching: 5   Yes ()   No (x)   Not sure ()

Comments: This website does not mail literature for free.

20. Does the website offer an interactive game to play?

Minutes searching: 2   Yes ()   No (x)   Not sure ()

Comments:

If yes, does the game provide further information about the destination and trip procedures to follow in visiting the destination?

Minutes searching: N/A

21. Can you find a photograph of a visitor at this website that looks like you?

Minutes searching: 6   Yes ()   No (x)   Not sure ()

Comments: The videos and slideshows all feature the Thai.

22. Can you information about what to do in case of a health or police emergency at this website?

Minutes searching: 4   Yes (x)   No ()   Not sure ()

Comments: Discusses assault, border issues, drugging, drug assaults, scams, theft and fraud, touts, and deep south assault in detail. Also lists great information on vaccinations, medication, a medical checklist, and insurance.

23. Does the website include specific information about shopping and specific stores to buy luxury goods?

Minutes searching: Yes ()   No (x)   Not sure ()

Comments: If you buy a tourism guide, the information is listed there. Lonely planet pushes endlessly for the purchase of their guides.

24. Does the website allow buying of specific products offered by specific stores via this official website?

Minutes searching: 5   Yes ()   No (x)   Not sure ()

Comments: It does suggest a shopping guide for purchase.

25. Does the website tell about the night clubs and night life?

Minutes searching: 5   Yes ()   No (x)   Not sure ()

Comments: Again, if you purchase a tourism book, this information is included.

26. Does the website permit booking to specific night clubs and night life events?

Minutes searching: 4   Yes ()   No (x)   Not sure ()

Comments: If you search within the site "Thailand nightclubs" a few safety precautions user comments result.

27. Does this website provide information for handicapped, impaired, visitors/customers/students?

Minutes searching: 5   Yes ()   No (x)   Not sure ()

Comments: It discusses in detail "getting around" but does not discuss any handicapped or impaired accommodations.

28. Is there a calendar of openings, holidays, closings, and/or special events at this website?

Minutes searching: 4   Yes (x)   No ()   Not sure ()

Comments: Closings specifically are not discussed.

29. Is current weather available as well as weather by month of year at this website?

Minutes searching: 12 Yes, current weather () Yes, for all months (x)
                       No current weather (x) No weather for each   Not sure ()
                                               month ()

Comments: The site lists "when to go" in terms of weather, differentiating between hot and rainy seasons. It suggests one travel between November and February, when it is neither too hot nor rainy.

30. Is the website available in languages other than English?

Minutes searching: 15 s   Yes (x)   No ()   Not sure ()

31. If yes, list all languages available at website:

English, Dutch, French, Spanish, Italian, Chinese, and Japanese

Comments: The icon is located at the bottom of the website "international."

32. Is historical information available at website?

Minutes searching: 1   Yes (x)   No ()   Not sure ()

Comments: There is an abundance of historical information on this site, dating back to prehistory and highlighting a number of historical events.

33. Is one or more slideshows of still photographs shown at the website?

Minutes searching: 4   Yes (x)   No ()   Not sure ()
Comments: Many pictures/slideshows were listed in this website.

34. Is one or more videos shown at the website?

Minutes searching: 1   Yes (x)   No ()   Not sure ()   If yes, how many videos?

Comments: Videos highlights specific aspects of tourism in Thailand.

35. Is safety/security information given at the website?

Minutes searching: 2   Yes (x)   No ()   Not sure ()

Comments: See above comments, site lists detailed information.

36. Does this website give visa requirements information?

Minutes searching: 1   Yes (x)   No ()   Not sure ()

Comments: The Thai government allows tourist-visa exemptions for 41 different nationalities, including those from Australia, New Zealand, the USA, and most of Europe, to enter the country without a prearranged visa. In 2008, the length of stay for citizens from exempted countries was slightly altered from years past. For those arriving in the kingdom by air, a 30-day visa is issued without a fee.

Russia Government Sponsored Rubric

Researcher's Name: Christopher P. Dion
Date: 4/05/2010

Website brand: Government sponsored
Website address: http://www.visitrussia.org.uk/

This site was all about applying for a visa. I checked another government sponsored Russian site (http://www.russia-tourism.ru/) and its links were not properly functioning. Not much information was available at all apart from trains, flights to Russia, hotels, and of course the visa. The only language available for each site was English (other than Russian). Overall it was a disappointment given that the other government sponsored sites feature ample and detailed information.

Issues:

Can I book a moderately priced hotel room at this website for a 10-day visit in mid-June 2010? ($150 per night)

Minutes searching for answer: 10   Yes (x)   No ()   Not sure ()

Comments: If you want to stay in a 5 star hotel, you will be paying more.

What do I get for this hotel room (free internet?; use of exercise room?; swimming pool?)

Minutes searching: 1   Not sure ()   1–3 amenities ()   4+ amenities (x)

Comments: 7 floors, 234 rooms, 2 restaurants, 2 bars, cafe, 3 conference halls, rooms for negotiations, fitness center, Lufthansa office, business center, exchange office, and parking.

3. Does the official site tell me what special events are available in mid-June 2010?

Minutes searching for answer: 12   Yes ()   No (x)   Not sure ()

Here is a detailed list of events in June:

4. If yes, can I book one of these events on-line at the official website?

Minutes searching: 2   Yes ()   No (x)   Not sure ()

Comments: (Describe events) N/A.

5. Can I become a "member" at this website? (If yes, do become a member if membership if free.)

Minutes searching: 2   Yes ()   No (x)   Not sure ()

Comments:

6. Can I pay to become a special member (e.g., pay dues) at this website?

Minutes searching: Yes ()   No (x)   Not sure ()

Comments:

7. What do I get for membership at the website?

Minutes searching: 2   N/A

Comments:

8. Does the website tell me what unique "must do" attractions that I should visit in June?

Minutes searching: 4   Yes ()   No (x)   Not sure ()

Comments:

9. Can I book one of these attractions at the official website?

Minutes searching: 2   Yes ( )   No (x)   Not sure ( )

Comments:

10. Does the website offer free paper copy literature that will be mailed to me?

Minutes searching: 4   Yes ( )   No (x)   Not sure ( )

Comments:

If yes, request this literature and record the date of the request and when you receive the literature. N/A.

11. Are videos shown at this website?

Minutes searching: 3   Yes (x)   No ( )   Not sure ( )

Comments: There are virtual tours of Moscow, St Petersburg, the Trans Siberian Railway, Golden Ring, Novgorod the Great, and the Sakhalin and Kurile Islands.

12. If yes, can I select a video that shows visitors doing things that I prefer to do at this destination?

Minutes searching: 3   Yes (x)   No ( )   Not sure ( )

Comments: Yes – visit St Petersburg, Moscow ride on the Trans-Siberian railway.

13. Can I see a map of the destination at the website?

Minutes searching: 2   Yes ( )   No (x)   Not sure ( )

Comments:

Can I request a map be sent to me via mail from this website?

Minutes searching: 4   Yes ( )   No (x)   Not sure ( )

Comments: You can "contact us" by phone, email, fax, Skype, or in person.

16. Can I book a classical upscale restaurant at the official website?

Minutes searching: 5   Yes ( )   No (x)   Not sure ( )

Comments: A table cannot be reserved here.

Minutes to book: N/A   Easy to do ( )   Hard to do ( )   Not sure ( )

Comments: N/A.

18. Does the website offer information for visits by families with young children?

Minutes searching: 4   Yes ( )   No (x)   Not sure ( )

Comments:

19. Can the visitor to the website ask for a mailing of literature about visiting for a family of two adults and two children 4 and 9 years old?

Minutes searching: 4   Yes ( )   No (x)   Not sure ( )

Comments: This website does not mail literature for free.

20. Does the website offer an interactive game to play?

Minutes searching: 2   Yes ( )   No (x)   Not sure ( )

Comments:

This website is all-visa, flights, hotels, and trains.

Minutes searching: N/A

21. Can you find a photograph of a visitor at this website that looks like you?

Minutes searching: 4   Yes ( )   No (x)   Not sure ( )

Comments: No.

22. Can you information about what to do in case of a health or police emergency at this website?

Minutes searching: 4   Yes ( )   No (x)   Not sure ( )

Comments:

23. Does the website include specific information about shopping and specific stores to buy luxury goods?

Minutes searching: 2   Yes ( )   No (x)   Not sure ( )

Comments:

24. Does the website allow buying of specific products offered by specific stores via this official website?

Minutes searching: 5   Yes ( )   No (x)   Not sure ( )

Comments:

25. Does the website tell about the night clubs and night life?

Minutes searching: 5   Yes ( )   No (x)   Not sure ( )

Comments:

26. Does the website permit booking to specific night clubs and night life events?

Minutes searching: 4   Yes ( )   No (x)   Not sure ( )

Comments:

27. Does this website provide information for handicapped, impaired, visitors/customers/students?

Minutes searching: 5   Yes ( )   No (x)   Not sure ( )

Comments:

28. Is there a calendar of openings, holidays, closings, and/or special events at this website?

Minutes searching: 10   Yes ( )   No (x)   Not sure ( )

Comments:

29. Is current weather available as well as weather by month of year at this website?

Minutes searching: 12   Yes, current weather ( ) Yes, for all months ( )
                         No current weather (x) No weather for each   Not sure ( )
                                                 month (x)

Comments:

30. Is the website available in languages other than English?

Minutes searching: 15 s   Yes (x)   No ( )   Not sure ( )

31. If yes, list all languages available at website:

English, Dutch, French, Spanish, Italian, Chinese, and Japanese

Comments: The icon is located at the bottom of the website "international."

32. Is historical information available at website?

Minutes searching: 1   Yes ( )   No (x)   Not sure ( )
Comments:

33. Is one or more slideshows of still photographs shown at the website?

Minutes searching: 4   Yes (x)   No ()   Not sure ()

Comments: Again the virtual tours.

34. Is one or more videos shown at the website?

Minutes searching: 1   Yes (x)   No ()   Not sure ()   If yes, how many videos?

Comments: See above comments for specific tour topics.

35. Is safety/security information given at the website?

Minutes searching: 2   Yes ()   No (x)   Not sure ()

Comments:

36. Does this website give visa requirements information?

Minutes searching: 6   Yes (x)   No ()   Not sure ()

Comments:

This site is all about the visa. It encourages you to apply on the site itself. Tons of info listed. Very focused on the visa.

Russia Private Sector Rubric

Researcher's Name: Christopher P. Dion
Date: 4/05/2010

Website brand: Lonely Planet (Global)
Website address: http://www.lonelyplanet.com/russia

Issues:

Can I book a moderately priced hotel room at this website for a 10-day visit in mid-June 2010? ($150 per night)

Minutes searching for answer: 10   Yes (x)   No ()   Not sure ()

Comments: Visiting this country is pricier than Poland and Thailand, but there were a handful of options under 150/night. Many more options, however, hovered over the 150/night price range. I picked Moscow as our city choice given that is where we would most likely start our visit.

What do I get for this hotel room (free internet?; use of exercise room?; swimming pool?)

Minutes searching: 1   Not sure ()   1–3 amenities ()   4+ amenities (x)

Comments: At the Radisson Royal Hotel Moscow, you get a restaurant, beauty salon, live music, Internet, a business center, and cable for $138/night.

3. Does the official site tell me what special events are available in mid-June 2010?

Minutes searching for answer: 12   Yes (x)   No ()   Not sure ()

Comments: It mentions that June through August is the best time frame to visit and do tourist activities, which is helpful. When we considered going here last November, we were highly deterred by the description of there being "at least a foot of packed snow" on the ground.

Here is a detailed list of events in June:

June
Glinka Festival (1–10 June) In the composer's hometown of Smolensk, an annual festival is held in Mikhail Glinka's honor.

Sadko Festival (first weekend in June) Held in Novgorod, this event offers traditional Russia folk music, games, and food.

Stars of the White Nights Festival (June) Involves general merrymaking and staying out late, as well as a dance festival in Russia's cultural capital, St Petersburg.

Tun-Payram (Opening-of-Summer-Pastures Festival) With traditional food, costumes, and sports, this festival is celebrated in Askiz, usually on the first or second Sunday of the month, and then in villages.

Ysyakh (around 22 June) Eat traditional food while watching local sports and spectacular costumed reenactments of battles near Yakutsk.

Interfest (www.moscowfilmfestival.ru) Russia's premier film festival is held in Moscow.

Grushinsky festivals Folk music festivals held in Samara.

4. If yes, can I book one of these events on-line at the official website?

Minutes searching: 2   Yes ()   No (x)   Not sure ()

Comments: (Describe events) Here are a few more general events: Deliver your wishes to Russia's very own Santa Claus in Veliky Ustiug, explore mountains in Yekaterinburg, take the Trans-Siberian railway, see Lake Balkal, the world's deepest lake, explore volcanic landscape in Kamchatka, go to Moscow's Red Square and see the Russian ballet, museums, go to restaurants, shops, and clubs. Some events and activities link to external websites.

5. Can I become a "member" at this website? (If yes, do become a member if membership if free.)

Minutes searching: 2   Yes (x)   No ()   Not sure ()

Comments: It's free to be a member.

6. Can I pay to become a special member (e.g., pay dues) at this website?

Minutes searching: Yes ()   No (x)   Not sure ()

Comments: It seems as though this is a free site.

7. What do I get for membership at the website?

Minutes searching: 2   Multiple perks (x)   No ()   Not sure ()

Comments: Get and share tips, find groups to travel with, save trip places and itineraries, rate and review places you've been.

8. Does the website tell me what unique "must do" attractions that I should visit in June?

Minutes searching: 4   Yes ()   No (x)   Not sure ()

Comments: Again it mentions June as being one of the best months to visit.

9. Can I book one of these attractions at the official website?

Minutes searching: 2   Yes ()   No (x)   Not sure ()

Comments: The website links to other websites.

10. Does the website offer free paper copy literature that will be mailed to me?

Minutes searching: 4   Yes ()   No (x)   Not sure ()

Comments: Travel guides can be purchased. You can sign up for an on-line newsletter as well.

If yes, request this literature and record the date of the request and when you receive the literature. N/A.

11. Are videos shown at this website?

Minutes searching: 3   Yes (x)   No ( )   Not sure ( )

Comments: There are multiple travel videos.

12. If yes, can I select a video that shows visitors doing things that I prefer to do at this destination?

Minutes searching: 3   Yes (x)   No ( )   Not sure ( )

Comments: Yes – visit St Petersburg, ride on the Trans-Siberian railway (this was my favorite video and one of the things I would truly want to do while visiting Russia), and a video about Russian food.

13. Can I see a map of the destination at the website?

Minutes searching: 2   Yes (x)   No ( )   Not sure ( )

Comments: Click on "show map."

Can I request a map be sent to me via mail from this website?

Minutes searching: 4   Yes ( )   No (x)   Not sure ( )

Comments: You have to buy literature on this website.

16. Can I book a classical upscale restaurant at the official website?

Minutes searching: 5   Yes ( )   No (x)   Not sure ( )

Comments: A table cannot be reserved here.

Minutes to book: N/A   Easy to do ( )   Hard to do ( )   Not sure ( )

Comments: N/A.

18. Does the website offer information for visits by families with young children?

Minutes searching: 4   Yes ( )   No (x)   Not sure ( )

Comments: No but you can "walk in Pushkin's footsteps at his family estate" – no mention of activities for families.

19. Can the visitor to the website ask for a mailing of literature about visiting for a family of two adults and two children 4 and 9 years old?

Minutes searching: 4   Yes ( )   No (x)   Not sure ( )

Comments: This website does not mail literature for free.

20. Does the website offer an interactive game to play?

Minutes searching: 2   Yes ( )   No (x)   Not sure ( )

Comments:

If yes, does the game provide further information about the destination and trip procedures to follow in visiting the destination?

Minutes searching: N/A

21. Can you find a photograph of a visitor at this website that looks like you?

Minutes searching: 4   Yes ( )   No (x)   Not sure ( )

Comments: No.

22. Can you information about what to do in case of a health or police emergency at this website?

Minutes searching: 4   Yes (x)   No ( )   Not sure ( )

Comments: Again lonely planet does not disappoint here – at the top of the overview, it mentions the heightened security following the two suicide bomb attacks in Moscow and links to "safe travel," which is a New Zealand safety link, with ample and extensive information in regard to which areas are the most dangerous. This also links to the US Department of State, which again has extensive precautionary information upon traveling in Russia, health and police emergencies. On the right hand side, there are also "Current Travel Warnings, Current Travel Alerts and Country Specific Information."

23. Does the website include specific information about shopping and specific stores to buy luxury goods?

Minutes searching: 2   Yes ( )   No (x)   Not sure ( )

Comments: If you buy a tourism guide, the information is listed there.

24. Does the website allow buying of specific products offered by specific stores via this official website?

Minutes searching: 5   Yes ( )   No (x)   Not sure ( )

Comments: It does suggest a guide for purchase.

25. Does the website tell about the night clubs and night life?

Minutes searching: 5   Yes ( )   No (x)   Not sure ( )

Comments: Again, if you purchase a tourism book, this information is included.

26. Does the website permit booking to specific night clubs and night life events?

Minutes searching: 4   Yes ( )   No (x)   Not sure ( )

Comments: If you search within the site "Russia nightclubs" a few clubs are mentioned in specific areas, but you cannot book on the site.

27. Does this website provide information for handicapped, impaired, visitors/customers/students?

Minutes searching: 5   Yes ( )   No (x)   Not sure ( )

Comments: If you search through user comments and reviews, many describe Russia as not being handicapped-friendly, nor user-friendly for travelers with babies or strollers.

28. Is there a calendar of openings, holidays, closings, and/or special events at this website?

Minutes searching: 10   Yes (x)   No ( )   Not sure ( )

Comments: See #3 for more detail. Under "when to go" it does list all the major holidays and festivals. It also mentions that July and August are holiday months for Russia (which means securing train tickets at short notice can be tricky). It also mentions tons of ticks, biting mosquitoes and other biting insects being the worst during these months (as an aside).

29. Is current weather available as well as weather by month of year at this website?

Minutes searching: 12   Yes, current weather ( )   Yes, for all months (x)
                   No current weather (x)   No weather for each   Not sure ( )
                                        month ( )

Comments: The site lists "when to go" in terms of weather.

30. Is the website available in languages other than English?

Minutes searching: 15 s   Yes (x)   No ( )   Not sure ( )

31. If yes, list all languages available at website:

English, Dutch, French, Spanish, Italian, Chinese, and Japanese

Comments: The icon is located at the bottom of the website "international."

32. Is historical information available at website?

Minutes searching: 1   Yes (x)   No ()   Not sure ()

Comments: Not as much history for Russia is listed as is available for Thailand and Poland.

33. Is one or more slideshows of still photographs shown at the website?

Minutes searching: 4   Yes (x)   No ()   Not sure ()

Comments: Pictures/slideshows can be found in the same area as the videos.

34. Is one or more videos shown at the website?

Minutes searching: 1   Yes (x)   No ()   Not sure ()   If yes, how many videos?

Comments: See above comments for specific video topics.

35. Is safety/security information given at the website?

Minutes searching: 2   Yes (x)   No ()   Not sure ()

Comments: See above comments, site lists detailed, and relevant information. Also: worth noting: Many Caucasians and Central Asians have been murdered by skinhead gangs in Moscow and St Petersburg in the past few years. There now exists a climate of fear among ethnic minorities as well. It also warns against drinking the water in St Petersburg (health precaution). The police and other uniformed officials will also pickpocket you; the site warns against letting an officer take your wallet from you.

36. Does this website give visa requirements information?

Minutes searching: 6   Yes (x)   No ()   Not sure ()

Comments: As we have found in previous research, getting the Russian visa can be a headache. Below lists detailed information from the Lonely Planet:

Visas

Everyone needs a visa to visit Russia and it's likely to be your biggest single headache in organizing a trip there – allow yourself at least a month before you travel to secure one. There are several types of visa, but for most travelers, a tourist visa (single or double entry and valid for a maximum of 30 days from the date of entry) will be sufficient and getting this should be relatively straightforward. If you plan on staying longer than a month, it's advisable to apply for a business visa. Whatever visa you go for, the process has three stages – invitation, application, and registration.

Note that application and registration rules for trips to sensitive border regions, such as the Altai, Astrakhan, the Caucasus parts of Northern European Russia and Tuva are slightly different; see each of these chapters for specific details. Also, there are a few regions and places in Russia that for security reasons you will not be granted a visa.

Invitation

To obtain a visa, you first need an invitation. Hotels and hostels will usually issue anyone staying with them an invitation (or "visa support") free or for a small fee (typically around €20 to €30). If you are not staying in a hotel or hostel, you will need to buy an invitation – costs typically range from €15 to €35 for a tourist visa, depending on whether you require a single or double entry type and how quickly you need the invitation, and €45 to €270 for the various types of business visa. This can be done through most travel agents, via specialist agencies (see p000R0293) and on-line through: (lists sites)

Application

Invitation in hand, you can then apply for a visa at any Russian embassy. Costs vary – anything from US$50 to US$450 – depending on the type of visa applied for and how quickly you need it. Rather frustratingly, Russian embassies are practically laws unto themselves, each with different fees and slightly different application rules – avoid potential hassles by checking well in advance what these rules might be. A useful website is Everbrite's Russia, Belarus, and Ukraine Pages (members.aol.com/imershein/Page2.html) which has recent posts on the application situations at various embassies and consulates.

We highly recommended applying for your visa in your home country rather than on the road – indeed, the rule is that you're supposed to do this, although we know from experience that some embassies and consulates can be more flexible than others. Trans-Mongolian travelers should note that unless you can prove you're a resident of China or Mongolia, attempting to get visas for Russia in both Beijing and Ulaan Baatar can be a frustrating, costly and ultimately fruitless exercise.

Registration

On arrival in Russia, you should fill out an immigration card – a long white form issued by passport control; these are often given out in advance on your flight. You surrender one half of the form immediately to the passport control, while the other you keep for the duration of your stay and give up only on exiting Russia. Take good care of this as you'll need it for registration and could face problems while traveling in Russia – and certainly will on leaving – if you can't produce it.

You must register your visa within three working days of arrival. (You're not required to register for stays of less than three days.) If you're staying at a hotel, the receptionist should be able to do this for you for free or for a small fee (typically around €20). Note that the very cheapest places sometimes will not oblige. Novosibirsk is notorious for forcing visitors into overpriced hotels to get that registration stamp, so it makes a bad arrival point. Once registered, you should receive a separate slip of paper confirming the dates you'll be staying at that particular hotel. Keep this safe – that's the document that any police who stop you will need to see.

If staying in a home stay or rental apartment, you'll either need to pay a travel agency (anything from €20 to €70) to register your visa for you (most agencies will do this through a hotel) or make arrangements with the landlord or a friend to register you through the post office. See waytorussia.net/RussianVisa/Registration.html for how this can be done as well as for the downloadable form that needs to be submitted at post offices. Note, while registering at post offices in cities and large towns is likely to be straightforward, this procedure cannot be guaranteed in more remote places.

Depending on how amenable your hotel or inviting agency is, you can request that they register you for longer than you'll actually be in one place. Otherwise, every time you move city or town and stay for more than 3 days, it's necessary to go through the registration process again. There's no need to be overly paranoid about this but the more thorough your registration record, the safer you'll be. Keep all transport tickets (especially if you spend nights sleeping on trains) to prove to any over-zealous police officers exactly when you arrived in a new place.

Registration is a hassle but it's worth doing for peace of mind since it's not uncommon to encounter fine-hungry cops hoping to catch tourists too hurried or disorganized to be able to explain long gaps.

Types of Visa
Apart from the tourist visa, other types of visas could be useful to travelers.

Business Visa. A business visa is far more flexible and desirable for the independent traveler than a tourist visa. These can be issued for 3 months, 6 months or 2 years, and are available as single-entry, double-entry or multiple-entry visas. They are valid for up to 90 days of travel within any 6 month period.

To obtain a business visa you must have a letter of invitation from a registered Russian company or organization, and a covering letter from your company (or you) stating the purpose of your trip. The "Invitation" agencies listed above can make these arrangements.

Transit Visa. This is for "passing through" Russia, which is loosely interpreted. For transit by air, it's usually good for 48 h. For a nonstop Trans-Siberian Railway journey, it's valid for 10 days, giving westbound passengers a few days in Moscow; those heading east, however, are not allowed to linger in Moscow.

72-H On-Demand Visa. Valid for visits of up to 72 h, thus good for a long weekend, this visa is only available for the Kaliningrad region and allows you to skip the application step at a Russian embassy or consulate. It's also only available to citizens of certain countries. You need to apply at least a week in advance of your travel dates via specific travel agencies in the region; you'll then be met at the airport by a representative of the agency.

Visa Extensions & Changes
Any extensions or changes to your visa will be handled by offices of UFMS (Upravleniye Federalnoy Migratsionnoy Slyzhby), Russia's Federal Migration Service, often just shortened to FMS. It's likely you'll hear the old acronyms PVU and OVIR used for this office.

Extensions are time consuming, if not downright difficult; tourist visas can't be extended at all. Try to avoid the need for an extension by asking for a longer visa than you might need. Note that many trains out of St Petersburg and Moscow to Eastern Europe cross the border after midnight, so make sure your visa is valid up to and including this day. Don't give border guards any excuses for making trouble.

CONSUMER-GENERATED ADVERTISEMENTS: EXAMINING AND CREATING EXECUTIONS FOR STARBUCKS AND CHIPOTLE COMMERCIALS

Aimée C. Kaandorp

ABSTRACT

Consumer-generated advertisements are advertisements made by consumers for brands they love and hate. This study considers why consumers create their own brand commercials and how to classify the types of commercials they make. The chapter also discusses the attitude of companies toward consumer-generated advertisements and the effect of companies' attitudes on the commercials. The study compares two different brands with a different attitude toward consumer-generated advertisements – Starbucks and Chipotle. An active and positive attitude of the company toward consumer-generated advertisements results in more positive advertisements.

Tourism-Marketing Performance Metrics and Usefulness Auditing of Destination Websites
Advances in Culture, Tourism and Hospitality Research, Volume 4, 139–147
Copyright © 2010 by Emerald Group Publishing Limited
All rights of reproduction in any form reserved
ISSN: 1871-3173/doi:10.1108/S1871-3173(2010)0000004011

INTRODUCTION

The creation of advertisements is no longer the privilege of companies only, but consumers are crafting and broadcasting them as well. This study finds that consumers generate different types of advertisements, and firms may respond to this phenomenon in different ways.

This study investigates various advertisements that consumers make and the motivations affecting consumers to create them. Different types of advertisements require different types of actions from the companies that are subject of these commercials. If advertisements are positive, the brand is probably benefiting from the consumer-generated advertisement. If the advertisement is negative, this might have a negative impact on the whole image of the company. Because the phenomenon of consumer-generated advertisements is rather new, managers have difficulties understanding what the right actions are to take (Berthon, Pitt, & Campbell, 2008, pp. 6–8).

This study compares consumer-generated ads for two different companies. One company, Chipotle Mexican Grill, runs contests for their consumers to generate advertisements for the company. The other company, Starbucks, does not hold contests for their consumers, but many consumers created advertisements for Starbucks as well. The central question of this chapter is the following: "Does active involvement of companies result in more positive consumer generated advertisements?"

The section Literature Review provides more insight in consumer-generated advertisements. In the next section, the propositions are announced. After the propositions, the different consumer-generated advertisements of both Starbucks and Chipotle will be divided into categories and will be compared with each other and examined. In that part, there is a discussion about the results of the content analysis. The last part of this chapter will be the discussion part.

LITERATURE REVIEW

Since the creation of the website YouTube (an online video-sharing platform) and the immense popularity of this website, consumers have a phenomenal platform to show their consumer-generated ads to the rest of the world. After Google, YouTube is the most visited website in 2009 in the United States. There are currently competitors for YouTube, but none of them has emerged to become as big as YouTube is (Netcraft, 2010). One of the most viewed consumer-generated advertisements might be the video of a boy playing on an electric guitar with the comment, "I learned to play guitar with the guitar Masters Pro. Practice, Practice and get a copy of Guitar Masters Pro. That is how I did it." This video on YouTube is watched more than 71 million times and is a great promotion for the brand Guitar Masters Pro (YouTube, 2010). Although many consumer generated advertisements contain a positive message for the brand, they can be very negative toward the brand as well.

Consider three types of advertisements consumers create. The first type of advertisement consumers could create is the "Hobbyist Ad." This ad is produced because of the intrinsic enjoyment it creates for the maker of the advertisement. The consumer wants to explore the product, and the ad is usually informative. This type of ad is usually created for brands consumers have high involvement in (Berthon et al., 2008, p. 17).

The second type of advertisements consumers could create is the so-called Me Ad. This ad is created to piggy-back on the brand or company and the main reason why consumers would create this ad is self-promotion. The focus of the advertisement is more on the creator of the ad rather than the brand itself. Humor and parody are frequently used, but not necessarily on the expense of the brand or company. This type of advertisement is often made for brands or companies that rule the media (Berthon et al., 2008, p. 17).

The third type of advertisements created by consumers is the "Activist Ad." This ad is composed by the motivation to change the perception of the viewers. The maker wants to promote or disrupt the brand. The creator does not want to promote himself. Humor and parody are often used and if the maker of the ad wants to disrupt the brand, the humor and parody is likely to be on the expense of the brand or company. The brands that are used in these consumer-generated ads are brands that consumers view as in need of support or disingenuous (Berthon et al., 2008, p. 17).

Because the phenomenon of consumer-generated advertisements is quiet new, managers often do not know what the best reaction of the company could be. On YouTube, some consumer-generated advertisements generate more than a million hits on the Internet, so their reach is significant. Others do not draw that much attention and are considered less successful in terms of awareness.

By and large, four categories of reactions by firms toward consumer-generated advertisements can be differentiated. The first possible reaction is to repel; this reaction is negative, and the response is active. This could be showed in suing the person who created the ad or writing a very desist letter to the creator (Berthon et al., 2008, pp. 10–11).

The second reaction that a firm can have is "disapproving." When the attitude of the company toward the advertisement is disapproving, the companies' reaction is negative, but the brand does not undertake action. This can range from blissful ignorance to reluctant tolerance.

The third attitude is the applaud response. If firms have this reaction, their reaction is both passive and positive. This approach is hands-off: no action is taken to facilitate or co-opt the creators of the advertisement (Berthon et al., 2008, p. 13).

The fourth approach is the facilitate approach. The firms' attitude toward consumer-generated advertisements is positive, and the reaction of the firm is active. The approach is "hands-on" and companies encourage their consumers to make advertisements for them, by means of contests for the best advertisement (Berthon et al., 2008, p. 13).

All these four options have their advantages and disadvantages. To determine whether the facilitate approach has a positive impact on the message consumers expose in their consumer-generated advertisements; this study compares the consumer-generated advertisements of two firms. The first firm has a facilitate approach, and the second firm has the disapproving approach. Eighteen different consumer-generated advertisements are criticized. The first company is the restaurant Chipotle Mexican Grill, opened in 1993 with the goal of serving fresh, gourmet-quality food at reasonable prices. Chipotle has tried to take an advantage of social networks. Chipotle offered a $30,000 prize to the universities or college teams that could produce the best Chipotle advertisement. Many of the advertisements ended up on YouTube. This is one of the reasons why Chipotle spends less than 1 percent of their budget on advertising, where the average spending on advertisements of restaurants is around 4 percent (Kotler, Bowen, & Makens, 2010, pp. 3–5). So, the approach of Chipotle Mexican Grill toward consumer-generated advertisements is both active and positive.

The other company is Starbucks. The customer loyalty of the company is rather high compared to other companies in the industry. The coffeehouse does not just sell coffee; they sell *The Starbucks Experience*, and they try to provide a "third place" outside the home and the office (Kotler et al., 2010, pp. 197–198). Berthon et al. (2008) state that Starbucks did not responded at all when a consumer-generated advertisement with a very negative attitude towards the brand was released on YouTube.

PROPOSITIONS

For Starbucks, 10 consumer-generated advertisements are selected. For Chipotle, eight consumer-generated advertisements are selected. The advertisements are divided per brand and per amount of views. There is one category for advertisements with less than 4,000 hits (five in both categories) and one category with more than 50,000 views. For the second category, five advertisements of Starbucks are studied and another three advertisements of Chipotle will be reviewed. There are only three Chipotle advertisements because there are only three consumer-generated advertisements on YouTube that received more than 50,000 views.

The first assumption is that the advertisements that are created for Chipotle Mexican Grill have generally a more positive attitude towards the brand than the advertisements made for Starbucks, because of the contest Chipotle held.

The second proposition is that there is no relationship between the length a consumer-generated advertisement has on YouTube and the magnitude of hits that commercial has. Some popular videos, like the Guitar Master Pro commercial, are relatively long (5 min and 22 s) compared to regular commercials.

The third statement is that there are more "Me-Ads" created for Chipotle than for Starbucks. The commercial contest of Chipotle would probably generate more advertisements in favor of the brand without too much information about the brand, not created from an intrinsic motive. The commercials would not be made on the expense of the brand either.

RESULTS

When you search for "Chipotle" on YouTube, you will find 4,210 hits. If you search for "Chipotle commercial," you will find 165 results. When you search for "Starbucks" you will find 46,700 hits. If you are looking for "Starbucks Commercial," you will find 1,010 results. These results are found on May, 4, 2010. Although Chipotle Mexican Grill ran the contest and Starbucks did not, there are significantly more movies and advertisements on YouTube about Starbucks. An explanation for this could be that the consumer-generated advertisements for the Chipotle contest are already removed from the YouTube channel.

The study uses a content analysis to test the hypotheses. A content analysis is used to provide a scientific, objective, systematic, quantitative, and generalizable description of communications content. A content analysis needs to be objective, so that different analysts may apply to the same body of content and secure the same results (Kassarjian, 1977, pp. 10–13).

On the basis of the propositions, this study compares the different advertisements according to different attributes. The different attributes are:

- Times watched (on May 4, 2010);
- Length of the consumer-generated advertisement;
- Attitude of the commercial toward brand (positive/negative);
- The implied values of the commercial;
- The type of advertisement (based on the three types mentioned in the literature review);
- Is humor used?
- Is there a slogan that comes with the commercial?
- Is music used?

All the advertisements are tested with these attributes. Four different tables result from all four categories of results from the content analysis. Table 1 shows the result of the advertisements about Starbucks with more than 50,000 hits. Table 2 shows the advertisements of Chipotle with more than 50,000 hits. Table 3 shows the results of the third category: the Starbucks consumer-generated advertisements with less than 4,000 views, followed by Chipotle's one with less than 4,000 views (Table 4).

The first proposition was that the consumer-generated advertisements for Chipotle do have a more positive attitude towards the brand than the commercials of Starbucks. This proposition is true, because none of the commercials about Chipotle have a negative attitude towards the brand, whereas two of the commercials about Starbucks have a negative attitude towards the brand. In these commercials, the creators also use humor at the expense of the brand.

The second proposition "There is no relationship between length of a commercial and the amount of hits the commercial generates" is not

Table 1. Consumer-Generated Advertisements > 50,000 Hits.

Name AD	Commercial	Commercial	Rap	Tall	Ad
Times watched	67,085	91,211	538,201	587,923	236,384
Length	1:20	0:31	2:43	3:06	0:47
Attitude toward	Positive	Positive	Positive	Negative	Negative
Implied values	Appreciation	Greedy	Creativity	Simplicity	Possession, health
Type of Ad	Hobbyist Ad	Hobbyist Ad	Me Ad	Activist	Activist
Humor?	No	No	Yes	At expense	At expense
Slogan	No	Yes	No	Yes	No
Music	Yes	Yes	Yes	No	Yes

Table 2. Chipotle Consumer-Generated Advertisements Watched > 50,000 Times.

Name Ad	Chipotle Rap	Chipotle Challenge	Burrito Make-Up
Times watched	262,243	57,574	131,355
Length	0:52	2:06	2:43
Attitude toward	Positive	Positive	Positive
Implied values	Appreciation	Power	Appreciation
Type of Ad	Me/Hobbyist	Me Ad	Me Ad
Humor?	Yes	No	Yes
Slogan	No	No	No
Music	Yes	No	Yes

Table 3. Starbucks Consumer-Generated Advertisements Watched < 4,000.

Name Ad	Hey Taxi!	Fake Starbucks Commercial	Starbucks	Good Coffee: Doing Good	The Coffee Monster
Times watched	1,172	1,395	1,745	816	1,744
Length	1:09	1:00	1:03	1:01	0:39
Attitude toward	Positive	Positive	Positive	Positive	Positive
Implied	Greedy	Happiness	Strength	Health, Success	Strength
Type of Ad	Me Ad	Me Ad	Me/Hobbyist	Me Ad	Me Ad
Humor?	Yes	No	Yes	No	Yes
Slogan	Yes	No	No	Yes	No
Music	Yes	No	Yes	Yes	No

entirely true. The means of the length of the advertisements of category 1 and 2 (both brands with more than 50,000 hits) are higher than the means of the advertisements of category 3 and 4 (both brands with less than 4,000 hits). The mean of category 1 is 101.4 s. The mean of category 2 is even higher, 113.67 s. The mean of category 3 is only 58.4 s, whereas the mean of category 4 is 65.2 s. The more popular commercials are almost twice as long as the less popular commercials. An expectation before the study was that the popular commercials have regular commercial time – between 30 and 60 s.

The third proposition stated that "The amount of Me Ads would be higher for Chipotle than for Starbucks." For Starbucks, five out of the ten commercials are labeled as Me Ads. For Chipotle, five out of eight commercials are labeled as Me Ads. For both brands, one advertisement is

Table 4.   Consumer-Generated Advertisements Chipotle
Watched <4,000.

Name Ad	Chipotle Commercial	Giant Burrito Pranks	Locate Your Soul Mate	Chipotle Ad	Chipotle Commercial
Times watched	3,985	1,979	349	3,732	2008
Length	1:06	0:58	0:30	0:35	2:17
Attitude toward	Positive	Positive	Positive	Positive	Positive
Implied values	Success	Appreciation	Simplicity possession	Beauty	Endurance
Type of Ad	Me Ad	Activist Ad	Me Ad	Hobbyist Ad	Me Ad
Humor?	Yes	No	Yes	Yes	No
Slogan	No	Yes	Yes	No	Yes
Music	Yes	Yes	Yes	No	Yes

labeled as both Me Ad and Hobbyist Ad. So, 75% of the consumer generated advertisements of Chipotle is named as a Me Ad, while only 60% of the consumer generated Ads of Chipotle are determined as Me Ads. This shows that the percentage of Me Ads is higher for Chipotle than for Starbucks and therefore, the third proposition can be seen as correct.

The attribute humor was important to see if the humor was at expense of the brand. Only for the two commercials that show a negative attitude towards the brand, we see that the humor is at expense of the brand. The tables show that the use of music and slogans is not relevant for the amount of hits and success of the consumer-generated advertisement.

DISCUSSION

The differences between the commercials created for both brands are not as big as expected on forehand. For both Starbucks and Chipotle, "Me-Ads" are created. The advertisement "Small is Tall" for Starbucks makes fun of the confusing size names of the cups. However, the message that is exposed is not extremely negative. For both brands, humor is used. The effects of humor are different for different levels of involvement with the brand. If the involvement with the brand of the viewers is low, the thoughts toward the brand are more favorable, but that does not change the attitude towards the brand. If the consumers are highly involved with the brand, the humor in the advertisements should add value to the message. Using humor in advertisements is an effective option in some contexts, but the involvement moderates the effect of humor (Zhang & Zinkhan, 2006, pp. 11–12).

This study shows that the length of the consumer-generated advertisements increases with the popularity of the commercials. The mean of the popular commercials was bigger than the mean of the less-attractive commercials. This was the case for both brands.

To conclude, the answer to the central question of this chapter "Does active involvement of companies result in more positive consumer generated advertisements?" is yes. For Chipotle, no negative commercials can be found on YouTube, while there are two negative consumer-generated advertisements with a significant amount of hits about Starbucks. For Chipotle in general, this study finds no negative commercial on YouTube. For Starbucks, more Activist Ads (most dangerous for image of brand) are created. This shows that the active involvement of Chipotle causes more positive consumer-generated advertisements than the passive involvement of Starbucks. However, much more clips for Starbucks are available on YouTube, despite the fact that Chipotle ran the contest.

REFERENCES

Berthon, P., Pitt, L., & Campbell, C. (2008). Ad lib: When customers create the ad. *California Management Review, 50*(4), 6–30.

Kassarjian, H. H. (1977). Content analysis in consumer research. *Journal of Consumer Research, 4*(1), 8–18.

Kotler, P., Bowen, J. T., & Makens, J. C. (2010). *Marketing for hospitality and tourism.* Upper Saddle River: Pearson Education Inc.

Netcraft. (2010). Available at http://toolbar.netcraft.com/stats/topsites

YouTube. (2010). Available at http://www.YouTube.com/watch?v=vFLs9RI8mSA&feature=related; http://www.YouTube.com/watch?v=VnbT7qt6RF4; http://www.YouTube.com/watch?v=4VWMVYibkfo&feature=related; http://www.YouTube.com/watch?v=xfOPYsk6nf4&feature=related; http://www.YouTube.com/watch?v=1qK5GZp4NAk&feature=related; http://www.YouTube.com/watch?v=wdjo8WCjHek; http://www.YouTube.com/watch?v=Yr5LfaG5fT8&feature=related; http://www.YouTube.com/watch?v=XWwK0h68TWM&feature=related; http://www.YouTube.com/watch?v=QXHa-dVZx7o&feature=related; http://www.YouTube.com/watch?v=4HNwT6-H-pM&feature=related; http://www.YouTube.com/watch?v=QLSDLdV26vM; http://www.YouTube.com/watch?v=kK4qINe4qyE&feature=related; http://www.YouTube.com/watch?v=BbqkSAppf8Q&feature=related; http://www.YouTube.com/watch?v=Clcf4QBupDI&feature=related; http://www.YouTube.com/watch?v=OEhteWJdgeg&feature=related; http://www.YouTube.com/watch?v=UHatsqtB5bY; http://www.YouTube.com/watch?v=eU9Y_2uNZG8; http://www.YouTube.com/watch?v=CiRPWP5sp1I&feature=related

Zhang, Y., & Zinkhan, G. (2006). Responses to humorous ads. *Journal of Advertising, 35*(4), 113–127.

TOWARD A BEHAVIORAL THEORY OF GOVERNMENT–FIRM RELATIONSHIP BEHAVIOR: THICK DESCRIPTION OF THE DYNAMICS OF GOVERNMENT'S ROLE IN SHAPING CHINA'S DOMESTIC, INBOUND, AND OUTBOUND TOURISM INDUSTRY

Songshan (Sam) Huang

ABSTRACT

This chapter describes and applies concepts informed by the behavioral theories of the firm to investigate the macrocosmic dynamisms as embodied in China's travel agency policy changes. Through a focused thick description, the study reviews the evolution of China's travel agency regulations since its reform and opening up era and subsequently discusses the impacts and implications of the recent changes in China's travel agency regulations on the regional tourism. By reviewing the evolution of China's travel agency regulations and discussing the impacts of the recent

Tourism-Marketing Performance Metrics and Usefulness Auditing of Destination Websites
Advances in Culture, Tourism and Hospitality Research, Volume 4, 149–163
Copyright © 2010 by Emerald Group Publishing Limited
All rights of reproduction in any form reserved
ISSN: 1871-3173/doi:10.1108/S1871-3173(2010)0000004012

changes in the 2009 Travel Agency Act on the regional tourism, this chapter demonstrates that (1) the government has undergone a learning process to integrate both internal and external evolution factors in regulating its travel agencies' behaviors; (2) the government–firm relationship behaviors remain the center in the evolution of China's travel agency policies; and (3) the 2009 Travel Agency Act would act as a shock factor initiated by the government to change the routines in firm behaviors, and subsequently the population ecology in both China's and the regional tourism industry.

INTRODUCTION

Policy changes along the time demonstrate the process of a governmental organization's decision making as a special form of organizational behavior. By examining the evolution of policy changes in an industry, one can hopefully gain a better understanding of how government–firm relations evolve and what determines the evolvement and eventually draw some meaningful conclusions on the patterns regarding government–firm relationship behavior.

Government–firm relationship behavior in the context of China's tourism industry is worth research exploration in several reasons: first, China has long been practicing a government-led tourism development strategy (Kuang, 2001), which enables the government a powerful position to regulate, direct, supervise, and control firms in its tourism industry; second, in comparison with western country governments, the Chinese government demonstrates a unique capacity in intervening its economic activities through policies, which is highlighted in the Chinese government's coping with the financial crisis in 2009; third, in a transition economy like China with a different cultural tradition from that of western countries, government–firm relationship behavior may have its own cultural roots and thus appears more intriguing.

This study borrows concepts inherited from Cyert and March's (1963) seminal work, *A Behavioral Theory of the Firm*, to examine the government–firm relationship behavior in China's tourism industry. The study provides a "thick description" of the dynamics of government's role in shaping China's domestic, inbound, and outbound tourism by tracing the policy changes of a core industry sector, the travel agency policies. Through the "thick description," the study also identifies and discusses some theoretical patterns.

Although the literature shows numerous research attempts to extend the theories in Cyert and March's (1963) book in various organization behavior areas, only a limited number of studies directed their attentions to public administration and policy making (e.g., Christensen & Lægreid, 2003; Olsen, 2003). Nevertheless, governmental agencies appear to be organizations whose behaviors are affected by their goals, which are largely defined and determined by government–firm relationships in their industry-related responsibilities. In this sense, some behavioral models may be more relevant in examining government–firm relationship behavior than others.

Learning theory and evolutionary economics as process-oriented models (Argote & Greve, 2007) may be more applicable to explain government–firm relationship behavior. These models concern how certain events and experiences factor in motion processes of decision making, routine development, or routine selection that change organizational behavior. The price and output model as specified by Cyert and March (1992), though not directly linked to government decision making, can also be applicable to firm's behaviors when studying government–firm relationships. In addition, two other key concepts or mechanisms are more useful to the present study: bounded rationality and population ecology (Argote & Greve, 2007). Bounded rationality characterizes the firm as an adaptively rational system rather than an omnisciently rational system. It assumes a number of states with the system. At any given time, the system prefers some states over others; and there exists external source of disturbance or shock that cannot be controlled to the system (Cyert & March, 1992). Population ecology explains the effects of legitimacy and competition on the evolution of industries and the life chances of individual firm (Hannan & Freeman, 1989). This study constantly revisits these relevant models and concepts when picturing the government–firm relationship behaviors under investigation.

STUDY BACKGROUND

As China becomes one of the most influential players in the world travel market, with its expected inbound and outbound tourism figures reaching 140 million and 100 million and ranking number 1 and number 4 respectively by 2020 as forecast by World Tourism Organization (UNWTO) (2001), changes of policies and industry practices originated in China will naturally exert a spill-over effect on the tourism development in other countries. Tourism over the years has been influenced greatly by globalization and in turn exerted its role in accelerating the process of globalization.

The tourism industry has been globalized than ever before. Thus, close observations and examination of shock factors created in one country and their impacts on other countries appear to be more appealing in tourism studies. The new travel agency act which has been put into effect since May 1, 2009, by the Chinese government has signaled significant changes in China's regulations on tour and travel related operations. The implementation of this new act is believed to have a "reshuffling" effect on the tourism industry in China (Wang, 2009) and thus can be treated in an academic sense as a shock factor employing the population ecology theory. As China has become Asia's leading tourist-generating market (Shao, 2008), the ripple effect caused by the "reshuffling" industry practices initiated by the new act would sooner or later be felt in the broader Asia Pacific tourism circles.

EVOLUTION OF TRAVEL AGENCY
REGULATIONS IN CHINA

In China, *luxingshe*, literally translated as "travel agency" in English, comprises all travel-related businesses approved by the government, including those conducted by a typical tour operator or a travel agency equivalent to that in western countries. After the founding of the People's Republic of China, travel agencies were mainly state-owned and state-operated. The first travel agency in the new People's Republic was Xiamen Overseas Chinese Service founded on October 17, 1949, which was at that time designated to receive and accommodate overseas Chinese and later became the state-owned China Travel Service (CTS). In April 1954, China International Travel Service (CITS) was set up with branch offices in 14 major cities (He, 1999). At that time, government surrogated travel agencies in their major business functions. For example, CITS functioned more like a government agency than a business enterprise or a firm in its modern sense. Thus, the government–firm relationship behavior was hard to define because there were lots of duplications of functions between the government and the "firm."

From 1949 to 1978, tourism was regarded as part of foreign affairs and most international tourism activities were in the form of "diplomatic reception" (Lew, Yu, Ap, & Zhang, 2003; Zhang, Pine, & Zhang, 2000; Zhang, Pine, & Lam, 2005). Accordingly, travel agencies predominantly played a political role in the country's foreign affairs. After China adopted its reform and opening-up policies in 1978, tourism began to gain a clearer industry status by acting as an economic contributor (Huang, 2010). At the same time, travel agencies in China experienced a rapid growth in number and began to see more independent business operations free from government intervention. In 1987, there were 1,245 travel agencies in China (He, 1999); by the end of 2007, the total number of travel agencies in China increased to 18,943, 15 times of the number in 1987 (China National Tourism Administration [CNTA], 2008). The propagation of travel agencies also marked a gradual clarification of the government–firm relationships in China's tourism industry.

Regulations and policies are the major actions and relationship behavioral formations between the government and travel agencies. With a relatively short history of regulating its travel agency industry, China has undergone two major revisions of its travel agency act. The first travel agency act, titled *Provisional Regulations on the Administration of Travel Agencies*, was promulgated by the State Council in July 1985. The act was China's first administrative legislation in tourism. In China's administrative legislation system, regulations issued by the State Council, normally in the name of the Premier, stand on the top of the system and are more powerful than regulations issued by ministries. Ministries can also issue ministerial regulations within their jurisdictions representing a lower level administrative legislation. In 1996, the travel agency act was revised and promulgated by the State Council; the title was changed to *Regulations on the Administration of Travel Agencies*. The most prominent difference between the 1985 Act and the 1996 Act was the classification of travel agencies and their business scopes, with the new version of the act being more detailed.

Under the 1985 Act, the travel agency classification includes three categories: Category I agencies can promote their businesses to overseas markets and receive overseas visitors; Category II agencies are not allowed to promote their businesses to overseas markets but can receive overseas visitors solicited though Category I agencies; Category III agencies can only deal with domestic tourism businesses demanded by Chinese citizens. Under the 1996 Act, only two categories of travel agencies were defined: international travel agencies (ITAs) and domestic travel agencies (DTAs). ITAs can operate inbound, outbound, and domestic tourism businesses, whereas DTAs can only operate domestic tourism businesses. However, in practice, only those ITAs licensed by the government can organize outbound package tours. Here we see the government–firm relationships were dominated more by the government through a licensing behavior. Without a license, travel agencies cannot operate a certain type of tourism business such as outbound travel.

The government's consideration and control of outbound tourism is obvious through the licensing system. In December 2001, the 1996 Act underwent a major revision in response to the World Trade Organization (WTO) membership commitments. The revision incorporated additional clauses regulating foreign and joint-venture travel agencies in China. Although the policy changes embodied in the 1996 Act as compared to the 1985 Act represent both the industry evolution process through incremental change and the government's adaptive learning to the gradual changing industry situation, the WTO membership in 2001 brought about an externally generated disturbance or shock factor that accelerated the government–firm behavioral transition. The result was the government's further loosening of some travel business operations, such as foreign travel agencies operating in mainland China.

Travel agencies in China belong to a highly regulated sector in the tourism industry. Even though the government has spent considerable effort in regulating such a sector, the industry practices are far from satisfactory. Starting from the mid-1980s, travel agencies proliferated due to the rapid development of domestic tourism. The number of agencies providing domestic travel services increased from fewer than 300 in 1984 to 7,725 in 2000. At the same time, travel agencies became more market-driven with the country's transition from a planned economy to a market economy (Zhang et al., 2005). Both the rise of number and the market-driven behavior of travel agencies during this period illustrate the effects of population ecology of the industry and organizational learning at the individual level. However, despite the government control, market disorder or chaos has been obvious in the industry. The most detrimental problem is that travel agencies compete with each other in an unhealthy way that may harm the whole industry. Other related problems or malpractices include subcontracting of departmental functions of travel agencies and illegal trade of outbound travel quota. These phenomena could be explained well by the behavioral theories of the firm. Examining how travel agencies react to formulate pricing strategies in coping with market competition would be separate study.

With the development of China's outbound tourism, the problems in China's travel agency sector have also been spread over to some major destination countries such as Thailand, Singapore, Malaysia, and Australia. A typical operational practice has been adopted by travel agencies in China in both their domestic and outbound businesses. The practice is literally labeled "zero package fee" (ZPF) or "negative package fee"(NPF) operation (Gu & Zhao, 2008; Zhang, Heung, & Yan, 2009). "Zero dollar tour" and "zero commission tour" are other terms to denote the same phenomenon in the industry. Such a practice enables travel agencies to set up a quoted package tour price that can roughly cover the direct costs of the package tour components (e.g., airline tickets, hotel accommodation) or even be lower than the cost level. Travel agencies employing such an operation mode would obtain its profits through shopping commissions during the tour. Such an unhealthy industry practice will eventually infringe tourists' rights and damage the image of China's travel agency industry, for in most cases, consumers are enticed, coerced, or even threatened to do shopping against their free will.

The ZPF or NPF operation reflects to some extent a type of market failure in the tourism industry. Some scholars assume that the popularity of such a malpractice also reflects the immature nature of the Chinese tourism market (Qi, 2005). For an emerging tourism market like China, consumers may prioritize price over other issues in making their decision to join a package tour. Over the years, the ZPF/NPF practice has incurred consumer complaints toward travel agencies. The malpractice also remains one of the significant industry problems that the CNTA would strive to resolve through policy measures. The ZPF/NPF highlights an industry-based problem that goes beyond government–firm relationships, for more stakeholders than the government and the firm have been involved in the process. Population ecology and learning theory in general could be applied to explain most travel agencies' adaptive firm behaviors. For example, Zhang et al. (2009) employed a game theory approach to simulate Chinese travel agencies' behaviors in adopting zero-commission tours.

Although the industry problems could be one major reason for the formation of the recent 2009 Travel Agency Act, entitled *Regulation on Travel Agencies*, other factors like the continuing administrative reform and the current social and economic situation in China, both as internal and as external evolution factors, may also have played a decisive role in the birth of the new act. As the CNTA Vice Chairman Du Jiang points out, the 2009 Travel Agency Act was formulated by the State Council under the nation's general guidelines of establishing a full-fledged and complete socialist market economy and following market economy principles and the development needs of China's travel agency industry; the new act intends to completely adjust and reform the travel agency industry structure, operations, services, management, and monitoring systems (Du, 2009). The following section elaborates on the major changes in the new act in comparison with its predecessors.

MAJOR CHANGES IN THE 2009
TRAVEL AGENCY ACT

In comparison with the previous 1996 Travel Agency Act and its revised version in 2001, a number of major policy changes are recorded in the 2009 Travel Agency Act (Table 1). With regard to the ZPF/NPF, while the 1996 act stated that travel agencies should not undertake unfair competition, the 1999 act explicitly states that "travel agencies should not solicit tourists

Table 1. Major Policy Changes between the 1996 Act and the 2009 Act.

Concerned Issue	1996 Act	2009 Act
ZPF/ZDT	Travel agencies should not engage in unfair competition	Explicitly states that "travel agencies should not solicit tourist through a quoted price below the cost level," "without consent from tourists, travel agencies should not provide any other paid services than those specified in the contract" (Clause 27) Specifies 14 items that should be included in the contract
Itinerary change	Did not regulate agency behaviors to modify itinerary	Agencies should not change the itinerary as agreed in the contract unless the change is caused by irreversible forces (Clause 33)
ZPF-related tour guide remuneration issues	No clause	Travel agency should sign a labor contract with tour guide and pay the guide at a salary level no lower than the local minimal salary standard (Clause 32) Travel agencies should not request tour guides to receive package tour groups without a due fee payment or with a lower-than-cost payment; neither should they request tour guides to cover any cost of receiving tour groups (Clause 34)
Entry requirements	Registered capital of no less than RMB 1.5 million for ITAs and of no less than RMB 300,000 for DTAs	Registered capital of no less than RMB 300,000 for all new establishments; possible return of 50% of the deposit of quality assurance fund (QAF)

through a quoted price below the cost level" and "without consent from tourists, travel agencies should not provide any other paid services than those specified in the contract" (Clause 27). In addition, the new act specifies 14 items for inclusion in the service contract agreed between the travel agency and the customer. These include places of departure, transit, and destination of the tour, arrangements and standards of transport and accommodation services, the content and time for each sightseeing activity in the itinerary, duration and times for tourists' free activities, shopping times and duration, and names of shopping premises arranged by the travel agency (Clause 28).

Although the 1996 act did not regulate travel agencies' behavior to modify the itinerary, the new act specifies that travel agencies should not change the itinerary as agreed in the contract unless the change is caused by unpreventable forces (Clause 33). Accordingly, legal liabilities of violating the above specifications are stated in the new act. The responsible tourism administration can admonish or fine the violators; in extreme cases the responsible tourism administration can revoke operating licenses. Through these measures, the ZPF/NPF or similar practices are listed illegal in the law, and the industry will be refreshed with due attention to and effort on service quality instead of inferior price drags.

Another problem in relation to ZPF/NPF is that tour guides are not paid by the travel agencies that employ them. Because travel agencies practicing ZPF/NPF have to keep their quoted package tour prices as low as possible, they would like the tour guide to be remunerated through shopping commission and/or tips, instead of a fixed salary. To resolve this problem, the new act stipulates that the travel agency should sign a labor contract with the tour guide or tour leader it hires, and pay him or her at a salary level no lower than the local minimal salary standard (Clause 32).

On the contrary, travel agencies should not request tour guides and tour leaders to receive package tour groups without a due fee payment or with a lower-than-cost payment; neither should they request tour guides or tour leaders to cover any cost of receiving package tour groups (Clause 34). These are the countermeasures dealing with the current practice that travel agencies levy a "head-count" fee on tour guides (Gu & Zhao, 2008). A travel agency would charge a "head-count" fee to the tour guide based on the size of the group, assuming that the larger the group, the more commission the tour guide would receive from leading the tour.

The new act lowers substantively the entry requirements for the setup of a travel agency. At the same time, the new act simplifies the setup procedure and executes a further decentralization on license approval by tourism authorities. Under the 1996 Act, setting up an ITA requires registered capital of no less than RMB 1.5 million, while setting up a DTA requires registered capital of no less than RMB 300,000. Under the 2009 Act, registered capital of RMB 300,000 is required for setting up a travel agency (Clause 6). Although the quality assurance fund (QAF) has been kept in the new act, this quality assurance obligation has been made less stressful to most travel agencies. Travel agencies that operate inbound and domestic travel businesses only need to deposit RMB 200,000 as QAF (Clause 13). The tourism authority should return 50% of the deposit to the travel agency on the condition that the agency has not incurred any violations within three years after fulfilling the deposit (Clause 17).

The new travel agency act demonstrates a routine change in the industry resulted by an enduring problemistic search by the government. The government has different goals in fulfilling its responsibilities in comparison with the firm. Different from travel agencies in its profit-driven and maximization behaviors, the government's behaviors are directed toward maintaining a healthy and well-developed industry while at the same time keeping the consumers generally satisfied. As China moves toward a more humanistic society, consumer rights or public interest will increasingly fill the government's policy agendas.

IMPACTS ON REGIONAL TOURISM

The new act on travel agencies will bring about a reshuffling effect on the travel agency industry in China. The 2009 Act further lowers the entry barriers for setting up a travel agency. Setting up a travel business is no longer a weary process that would cause much of the business owner's time and energy. China's Administrative Approval Law requires responsible government agencies to approve or disapprove an application within a specific time span. Under the 2009 Travel Agency Act, tourism authorities must make a decision to approve or reject an application of setting up a travel agency within 20 working days after receiving the application.

The lowered entry requirements for setting up a travel agency mean that entering the travel agency business is easier. However, being easy to enter the market does not necessarily mean it is equally easy to manage a newly developed travel business. With more small- and medium-size businesses expected to enter the industry, competition level would also increase. However, under the new legal system, travel agencies cannot resort to price competition to win out as any equal-to-cost or below-cost pricing would be illegal. Eventually, they should focus on "service quality" to survive the fierce competition with industry peers. Price-based competition could still be a weapon for larger travel agencies to squeeze those smaller or weaker ones out of the market, but such a weapon should not be abused to the extent of ZPF/NPF exercise. The 2009 Travel Agency Act in China is a significant event that could be a shock input to change the population ecology in the regional tourism.

With the boom of its outbound tourism, China is now the leading tourism source market for many Asia Pacific countries. Because most Chinese outbound tourism businesses would involve partner tour operators or travel agencies in destination countries, changes in China's travel agency regulations could influence those tour operators and travel agencies that operate inbound group tours from China in their home countries. Specifically, tour operators in destination countries may have to change their modes of operation or partnership with their Chinese partners, mainly because their Chinese partners have to change their own business behavior in accordance with their home country-based travel agency act. In this regard, even though the new travel agency act is only legally effective within the China legislative territory (excluding Hong Kong and Macao as they are special administrative regions), its indirect impacts on tour operators or tourism industries at large in the Asia Pacific region cannot be overlooked. In the past, unhealthy practices typical in China's tourism industry (e.g., ZPF/NPF) also prevailed in major destination countries to Chinese travelers, such as Thailand, Singapore, and to some extent, Australia.

The impacts of China's new travel agency act on tour operations in the Asia Pacific countries should be analyzed from a supply chain perspective. Starting from the direct impact of the Act on Chinese travel agencies, to keep their business practices within the new legal framework, China-based travel agencies will have to follow a crystallized itinerary or a contract. If a travel agency wants to arrange more shopping activities to get more commissions, it should clearly state all the pre-arranged shopping activities in the consumer contract. The agency may reduce the package price to a level that would make it not violate the law to attract more customers.

The agency may recover some of its profit from the shopping commissions, while at the same time risking loss of customers because of the inclusion of shopping activities in the itinerary. On the customer side, they may choose a package tour that includes more shopping activities but is at a low price level, or they have to pay more for a package tour with less shopping activities. The new act intends to increase the transparency of the transaction between a travel agency and its customers. The act attempts to eliminate a gray area where the agency can manipulate tour arrangement against customers' will.

In a short term, the new act enactment would leverage up the market price for China outbound travel products because those agencies operating ZPF or NPF would have to increase their price quotations, or else they will be fined or punished according to the new act. In effect, recent media reports in relation to the new act did confirm a general trend of price increase on the outbound market (Wang, 2009). Industry news also noted that during the Labor Day holiday in 2009, package tours to the Southeast Asia countries recorded the biggest price soar; specifically, package tours to Thailand and Australia have all witnessed a price jump (Chinanews, 2009). Thailand is one of the major outbound destinations for Chinese nationals. The ZPF practices have been frequently recorded in this market. Therefore, the impact of China's 2009 Travel Agency Act on the Thai tourism industry would be more obvious.

The immediate price increase in outbound tours to Thailand represents only a starting point for a series of chain effect. Package tours to Australia have been badly reputed for the "additional fee" operation. "Additional fee" represents an unfair term under which the travel agency levies a certain amount of additional charge to some consumer groups for reasons that: (1) these groups have limited shopping capacity in the destination; (2) they would like to report complaints to media; and (3) they are more likely to launch lawsuits toward the travel agency. These groups are listed as "Beijing residents," "older people," "children," and professionals like journalists, teachers, and lawyers. The additional fee could be several hundred to thousands of Chinese RMB Yuan. One impact of the 2009 Travel Agency Act on package tours to Australia is that major agencies organizing outbound tours to Australia have abandoned the "additional fee" operation and unanimously added a margin of 3,000 Yuan (approximately US$440) onto their quoted price of Australia tours (Chinanews, 2009).

The general price increase will lead to a tentative reduction on outbound tourism demand in the short future, in parallel with the effect of the current financial crisis; however, in the long term the Chinese outbound market demand is less likely to be curbed. The short-term rise of package tour prices will also affect the travel businesses of China's major destination countries. But the influence is marginal. Given the unclear world financial situation, the uncertainty of the Asia Pacific tourism may be attributed more to the world financial crisis than China's new travel agency act. On the contrary, it is also foreseeable that healthier industry practices in China's travel agency industry directed by the new act will be transferred to the overseas industry partners. When China-based travel agencies adopt a more "quality"-driven competition strategy, they will take the lead and pass the business ethics to their overseas partners.

Travel agencies organizing outbound package tours in China tend to be large in size, and they may be in a position to influence and convince their overseas partners to follow their dance steps (Pan & Laws, 2003). Generally speaking, although the new act comes out mainly because of industry problems within China, the Act's positive impact of fostering fair and quality-driven competitions on the Asia Pacific regional tourism is obvious in the long term.

CONCLUSION AND IMPLICATIONS

As China becomes an influential player in the world tourism market in terms of its domestic, inbound, and outbound tourism, changes in China's major tourism policies will exert a spill-over effect on the regional tourism in the Asia Pacific region. This chapter applies several concepts informed by the behavioral theories of the firm to investigate the macrocosmic dynamisms as embodied in China's travel agency policies changes. By reviewing the evolution of China's travel agency regulations and discussing the impacts of the recent changes in the 2009 Travel Agency Act on the regional tourism, the chapter demonstrates that (1) the government has undergone a learning process to integrate both internal and external evolution factors in regulating its travel agencies' behaviors; (2) the government–firm relationship behaviors remain the center in the evolution of China's travel agency policies; and (3) the 2009 Travel Agency Act would act as a shock factor initiated by the government to change the routines in firm behaviors, and subsequently the population ecology in both China's and the regional tourism industry.

Regulations on travel agencies in China remain the core part on China's tourism policy agendas. To date, three administrative regulations promulgated by the State Council, namely *Regulation on Travel Agencies*, *Regulation on the Administration of Tour Guides*, and *Administrative Measures on Chinese Citizens' Outbound Tourism*, are all related to core businesses or business components of travel agencies. In the future, the travel agencies industry could still be a highly government-regulated sector in China, as the mass tourism consumption will continue to take a form of package tour (Tisdell & Wen, 1991; Zhang, 1997).

The new travel agency act, effective since May 1, 2009, has targeted to resolve a series of industry problems that had hassled both the industry and the government for a long time. New clauses were added in the Act to specifically deal with industry malpractices such as ZPF or NPF. The new act seems to be more mature and well developed in comparison with its two predecessors. It intends to rectify some business practice problems in China's tourism industry, which cannot be easily resolved by a free market mechanism. As the Chinese government becomes more experienced in leading its economy, the question remains whether some good administrative practices, as referred to the China model or China pattern, can be adapted by other countries. This chapter points out that the new travel agency act in China may not only create a healthier competition environment within China's tourism industry; it could also influence the regional tourism development in a way that leads to a more transparent, fair, and quality-driven regional tourism market.

ACKNOWLEDGMENT

The author thanks Arch Woodside, Boston College, for his constructive comments on earlier versions of this chapter.

REFERENCES

Argote, L., & Greve, H. R. (2007). A behavioral theory of the firm – 40 years and counting: Introduction and impact. *Organization Science*, *18*(3), 337–349.

China National Tourism Administration. (2008). *The yearbook of China tourism statistics.* Beijing: China Tourism Press.

Chinanews. (2009). Implementation of the travel agency regulation in May foretells a 'storm' of outbound tour price soars. *Chinanews*, April 10. Available at http://www.chinanews. com.cn/cj/cytx/news/2009/04-10/1640569.shtml. Retrieved on July 2, 2009.

Christensen, T., & Lægreid, P. (2003). Administrative reform policy: The challenges of turning symbols into practice. *Public Organization Review*, *3*(1), 3–27.

Cyert, R. M., & March, J. G. (1963). *A behavioral theory of the firm.* Engllewood Cliffs, NJ: Prentice Hall.

Cyert, R. M., & March, J. G. (1992). *A behavioral theory of the firm* (2nd ed.). Malden, MA: Balckwell.

Du, J. (2009). Speech on the national training seminar for the regulation on travel agencies. Available at http://www.cnta.gov.cn/html/2009-4/2009-4-30-12-9-14258.html. Retrieved on May 22, 2009.

Gu, J., & Zhao, X. (2008). A study on the reasons and solutions for 'zero package fee' and 'negative package fee' phenomena in tourism. *Journal of Jiaozuo Teachers College, 24*(1), 44–46.

Hannan, M. T., & Freeman, J. (1989). *Organizational ecology*. Cambridge, MA: Harvard University Press.

He, G. (Ed.) (1999). *50 years of China's tourism*. Beijing: China Tourism Press.

Huang, S. (2010). Evolution of China's tourism policies. *International Journal of Tourism Policy, 3*(1), 78–84.

Kuang, L. (2001). *Study on government-led tourism development strategy*. Beijing: China Tourism Press.

Lew, A. A., Yu, L., Ap, J., & Zhang, G. (Eds). (2003). *Tourism in China*. New York: Haworth Hospitality Press.

Olsen, J. P. (2003). Towards a European administrative space? *Journal of European Public Policy, 10*(4), 506–531.

Pan, G. W., & Laws, E. (2003). Tourism development of Australia as a sustained preferred destination for Chinese tourists. *Asia Pacific Journal of Tourism Research, 8*(1), 37–47.

Qi, L. (2005). Analyze the phenomenon of zero fee tour package in Hainan. *Journal of Guizhou University of Technology (Social Science Edition), 7*(6), 39–42.

Shao, Q. (2008). Speech on the 2008 national tourism working conference. Available at http://www.cnta.gov.cn.html/2008-6/2008-6-2-21-18-35-163.html. Retrieved on January 29, 2009.

Tisdell, C., & Wen, J. (1991). Foreign tourism as an element in PR China's economic development strategy. *Tourism Management, 12*(1), 55–67.

Wang, Y. (2009). 'Labour Day' tours behind the price increase – The new travel agency act will bring tourists real package tour price. *CNTA WebNews*, April 24. Available at http://www.cnta.gov.cn/html/2009-4/2009-4-24-12-33-38066.html. Retrieved on May 22, 2009.

World Tourism Organization (UNWTO). (2001). *Tourism 2020 vision volume 7: Global forecasts and profiles of market segments*. Madrid, Spain: WTO.

Zhang, G., Pine, R., & Zhang, H. Q. (2000). China's international tourism development: Present and future. *International Journal of Contemporary Hospitality Management, 12*(5), 282–290.

Zhang, H. Q., Heung, V. C. S., & Yan, Y. Q. (2009). Play or not to play – An analysis of the mechanism of zero-commission Chinese outbound tours through a game theory approach. *Tourism Management, 30*(3), 366–371.

Zhang, H. Q., Pine, R., & Lam, T. (2005). *Tourism and hotel development in China: From political to economic success*. New York: Haworth Hospitality Press.

Zhang, W. (1997). China's domestic tourism: Impetus, development and trends. *Tourism Management, 18*(8), 565–571.